MW00576699
THE ASTROLOGY DIARY 2024
ANA·LEO

THIS DIARY BELONGS TO

NAME

DATE OF BIRTH TIME

PLACE OF BIRTH STATE

SOLAR SIGN RISING SIGN

ADDRESS

CITY STATE

COUNTRY

PHONE MOBILE

EMAIL

WWW

The Astrology Diary 2024

First published in UK and USA in 2023 by
Watkins, an imprint of Watkins Media Limited
Unit 11, Shepperton House, 89–93
Shepperton Road, London N1 3DF
enquiries@watkinspublishing.co.uk

Author: Ana Leo
Designer: Maria Clara Voegeli
Illustrations: Shutterstock
Commissioning Editor: Lucy Carroll
Assistant Editor: Brittany Willis

ISBN: 978-178678-757-6

Printed in China

Signs of the Zodiac:

♒ Aquarius	20 January–17 February
♓ Pisces	18 February–19 March
♈ Aries	20 March–19 April
♉ Taurus	20 April–20 May
♊ Gemini	21 May–20 June
♋ Cancer	21 June–21 July
♌ Leo	22 July–22 August
♍ Virgo	23 August–21 September
♎ Libra	22 September–22 October
♏ Scorpio	23 October–21 November
♐ Sagittarius	22 November–20 December
♑ Capricorn	21 December–19 January

Hello,

AND WELCOME TO THE FOURTH EDITION OF THIS FANTASTIC ASTRAL MANIFESTATION MANUAL!

The idea for this diary started in 2018, when I was studying at the Faculty of Astrological Studies in Oxford, England. Every class I attended surprised me with so much new and powerful information, but I didn't have a guide to check the pace of the planets every month, every year. No such guide existed at the time. The following year, I independently published the first edition of *The Astrological Diary* in Brazil. And it was a much greater success than I expected.

This diary is for anyone seeking self-knowledge, self-care, and wanting to learn how to manage their internal tools and become their own gurus.

With every edition I reinvent myself and present to you a little more of what I have studied This year, 2024, is beyond special. The diary is increasingly becoming like an astrological and natural magick manual so that you can, with your own energy, transform your life according to the music of the Universe.

Tarot, Kabbalah, runes, rituals and sacred altars – they all connect us with our primordial essence, and take us back to a time when nature was our compass, when we could read more clearly the messages from the stars.

I hope I can help you reveal the light within you, so that you can direct your energy and take control of your life, using your inner power to your advantage, to become the creator of your own destiny.

We are all cosmic dust, beloveds.
Let's go together on this journey here on Earth.

Ana Leo

SIGNS

ARIES

TAURUS

GEMINI

CANCER

LEO

VIRGO

LIBRA

SCORPIO

SAGITTARIUS

CAPRICORN

AQUARIUS

PISCES

PLANETS

SUN

MOON

MERCURY

VENUS

MARS

JUPITER

SATURN

URANUS

NEPTUNE

PLUTO

ELEMENTS AND ASPECTS

FIRE

EARTH

AIR

WATER

CONJUNCTION
0°

SQUARE
90°

SEXTILE
60°

TRINE
120°

OPPOSITION
180°

℞
RETROGRADE

DIRECT

St
STATION

MY ASTRAL CHART

GO TO ASTRO.COM AND MAKE YOUR FREE CHART. COPY THE POSITION OF EACH PLANET INTO THIS GRAPHIC. YOU'RE STARTING TO GET IN TOUCH WITH EVERY ASPECT OF YOUR BIRTH CHART.

☉	☽	☿	♀	♂	♃	♄	♅	♆	♇	☊	☋
SUN	MOON	MERCURY	VENUS	MARS	JUPITER	SATURN	URANUS	NEPTUNE	PLUTO	NORTH NODE	SOUTH NODE

☉ ______

☽ ______

☿ ______

♀ ______

♂ ______

♃ ______

♄ ______

♅ ______

♆ ______

♇ ______

☊ ______

☋ ______

SOLAR & LUNAR CALENDARS

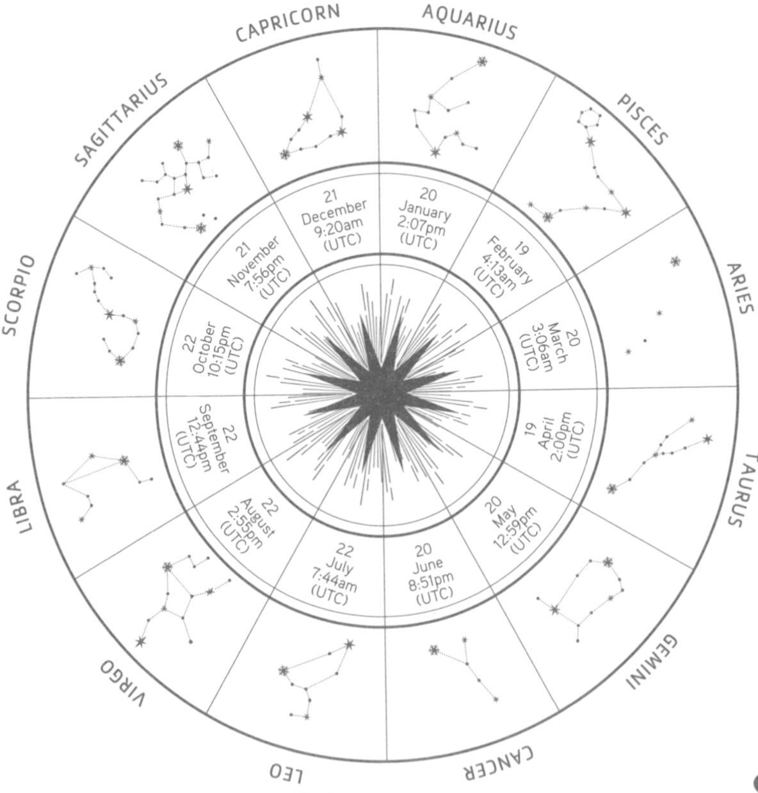

CAPRICORN — 21 December 9:20am (UTC)

AQUARIUS — 20 January 2:07pm (UTC)

PISCES — 19 February 4:13am (UTC)

ARIES — 20 March 3:06am (UTC)

TAURUS — 19 April 2:00pm (UTC)

GEMINI — 20 May 12:59pm (UTC)

CANCER — 20 June 8:51pm (UTC)

LEO — 22 July 7:44am (UTC)

VIRGO — 22 August 2:55pm (UTC)

LIBRA — 22 September 12:44pm (UTC)

SCORPIO — 22 October 10:15pm (UTC)

SAGITTARIUS — 21 November 7:56pm (UTC)

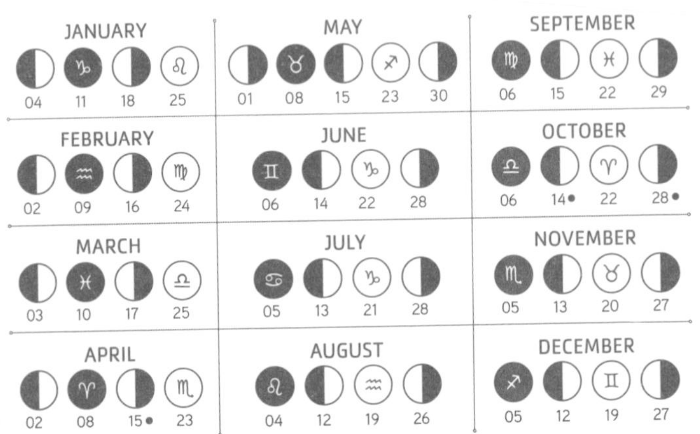

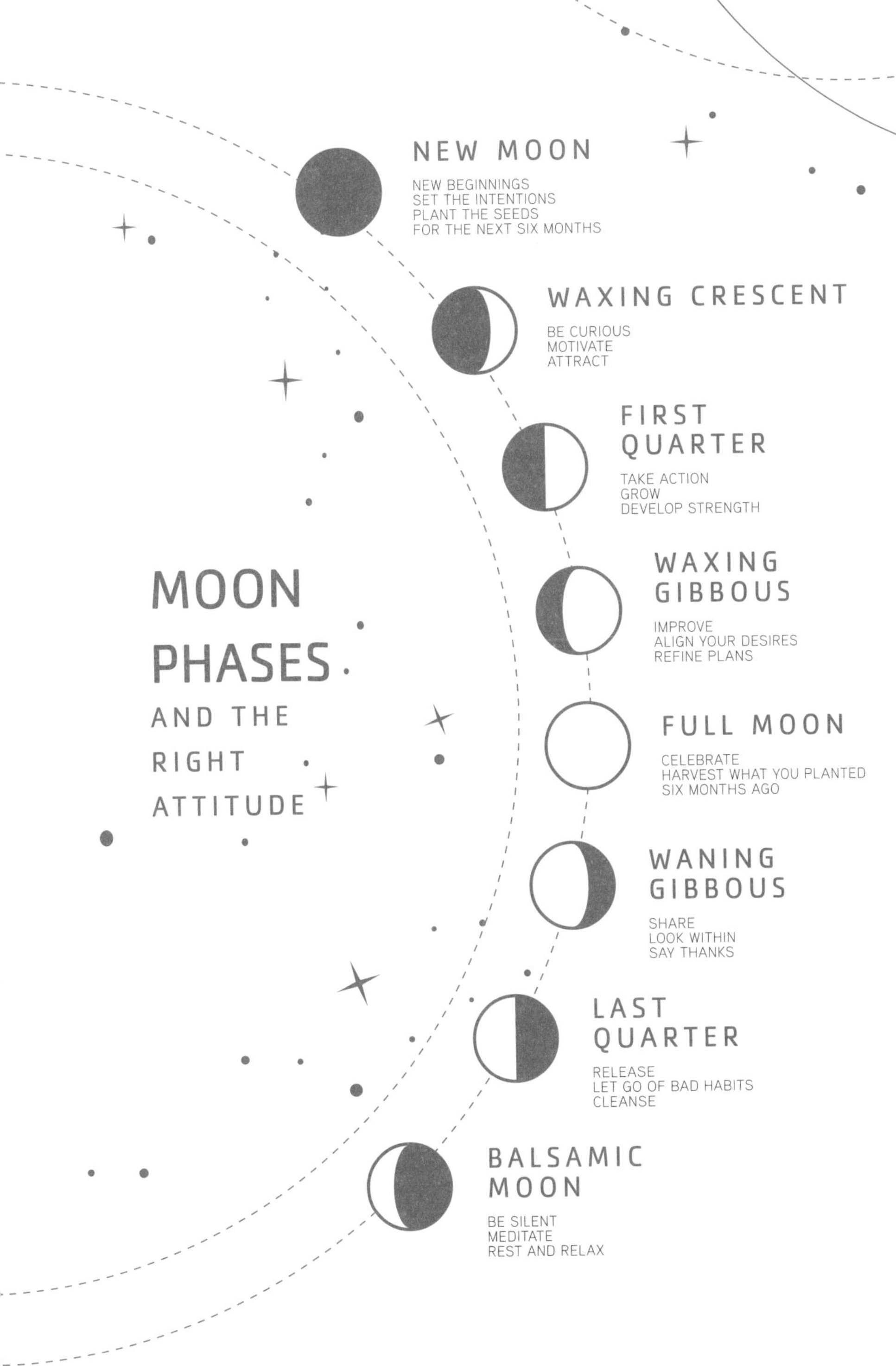
NEW MOON
NEW BEGINNINGS
SET THE INTENTIONS
PLANT THE SEEDS
FOR THE NEXT SIX MONTHS
WAXING CRESCENT
BE CURIOUS
MOTIVATE
ATTRACT
FIRST QUARTER
TAKE ACTION
GROW
DEVELOP STRENGTH
MOON PHASES AND THE RIGHT ATTITUDE
WAXING GIBBOUS
IMPROVE
ALIGN YOUR DESIRES
REFINE PLANS
FULL MOON
CELEBRATE
HARVEST WHAT YOU PLANTED
SIX MONTHS AGO
WANING GIBBOUS
SHARE
LOOK WITHIN
SAY THANKS
LAST QUARTER
RELEASE
LET GO OF BAD HABITS
CLEANSE
BALSAMIC MOON
BE SILENT
MEDITATE
REST AND RELAX

RETROGRADE PLANETS - 2024

MERCURY **13 DEC 2023–3 JAN / 8° ♑–22° ♑**

URANUS **28 AUG 2023–28 JAN / 23° ♉–19° ♉**

MERCURY **1 APR–25 APR / 27° ♉–15° ♉**

PLUTO **2 MAY–2 SEP / 2° ♒–29° ♑**

SATURN **29 JUN–15 NOV / 19° ♓–12° ♓**

NEPTUNE **2 JUL–7 DEC / 29° ♓–27° ♓**

MERCURY **5 AUG–28 AUG / 4° ♍–21° ♍**

URANUS **1 SEP–30 JAN 2025 / 27° ♉–23° ♉**

JUPITER **9 SEP–4 FEB 2025 / 21° ♉–11° ♉**

MERCURY **26 NOV–15 DEC / 8° ♑–22° ♐**

MARS **6 DEC–23 FEB 2025 / 25° ♊–8° ♊**

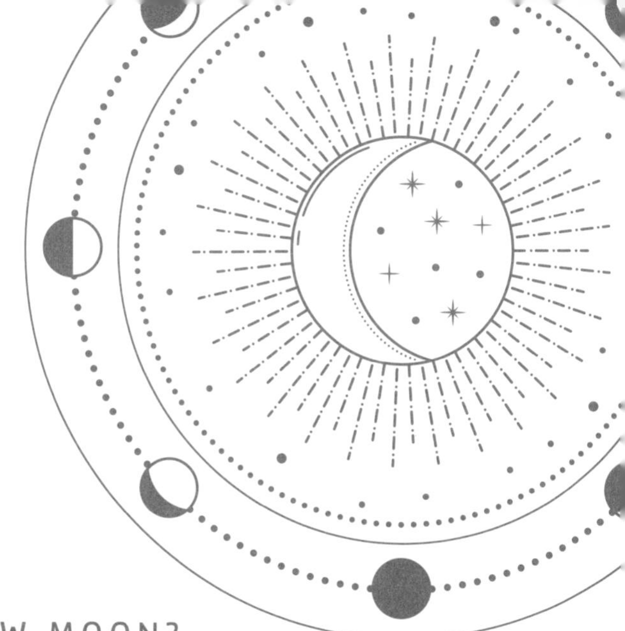

WHAT IS THE NEW MOON?

Every month, the Sun and Moon meet in the sky. This meeting is undoubtedly the most powerful moment in the entire lunar cycle, as it contains the perfect energy to start a new chapter.

During the New Moon, the Sun and Moon are in the same mathematical degree in the Zodiac. Together they join forces to help us work for our intentions. It is this unity that creates a powerful vibration in the Universe and within each one of us. Our strength and emotion are together, as if an energetic and cosmic portal has been opened, and we are invited to sow a seed of what we need to manifest in our lives. So the New Moon is the perfect time to take a first step or start a project, because the energy of the Moon is so strong that we can direct it to make great energetic leaps in our lives.

At the Full Moon we observe our entire journey in the last six months. It is the culmination of the events that emerged at the New Moon. It is when the Sun is on the opposite side of the Moon, illuminating her conquests and opposing her energy. Use the two weeks after New Moon to walk toward your goal and observe the first steps of your intentions. Work hand in hand with these cycles, so that in six months, when the Full Moon finally happens in that same sign, you will have manifested a new reality in your life.

Besides giving us the opportunity to start something, the New Moon also allows us an opening to balance our entire internal being: our soul, mind and spirit. Through the union of the Sun and the Moon, every month we have a new opportunity to create balance in our internal and external energies and, consequently, in our lives.

HOW TO MAKE MOST OF THIS MOMENT?

When the Sun and Moon are balanced, so are we. Each month, this diary will show you the ideal "theme" to work on, both in terms of your feelings and your actions.

The house on the astral chart, where the New Moon takes place, gives us clues, showing us the area of our life where we must put all our intentions in motion.

The New Moon pages in this diary were created to guide you in the use of these energies and to help you identify the areas to be worked on. In some months you will be more motivated to act; in others, you will be helped to vibrate what you want to feel.

Through the lens of the Zodiac, we are able to identify the right time to take action to transform our reality. The balance of these two vital energies is the key. When the two celestial bodies - the two most important luminaries for our daily life - come together in the sky to balance their energies, we must balance ours too.

HOW TO MANIFEST?

RULES TO SHOW YOUR INTENTIONS TO THE UNIVERSE

The exact moment of the New Moon possesses the greatest energetic force, so it is a time when you can plant your intentions for the next cycle.

The 12 hours before this event are charged with this energy and must be used, both for introspection and for reflection. Six months separate a New Moon from a Full Moon, in the same sign.

This is the period when we see our desire grow. Following its development, it is time to take care of it and give the necessary attention so that it manifests itself. Remember that your desire is like a seed that needs to be nourished every day, so that it grows and bears flowers and fruits. Just creating the list and not taking any action to make it a reality will not lift it off the paper.

Put at least five intentions on your list, always pointing out the necessary action for it to become reality. For example: I intend to lose 5kg (11lb) – I will start walking three times a week. I intend to get a job – I will rewrite my resumé and send it to a specific company I want to work for.

Make sure that you are asking a request from your soul, not your ego. The soul's desires require patience and dedication, and bring you long-term satisfaction. The ego's desires are superficial and only benefit you; your satisfaction is immediate and does not last for long.

Remember that you must feel as if you are already fulfilling all your wishes, so when you write them, imagine yourself as if they were already a reality. How would you feel? What would you say to other people? How would you describe it to the person who most wants to see your success? The greater the detail in your imagination, the better.

WHICH TIME ZONE IS CONSIDERED?

THIS DIARY CAN BE USED IN ALL COUNTRIES WITH THE FOLLOWING CONSIDERATIONS

All the time zones are described on the New Moon pages.
PST – Pacific Standard Time or PDT - Pacific Daylight Time
CST – Central Standard Time or CDT - Central Daylight Time
EST – Eastern Standard Time or EDT - Eastern Daylight Time
GMT – Greenwich Mean Time or IST/BST - Irish/British Summer Time
CET – Central European Time or CEST - Central European Summer Time

All the information in this diary has the intention of alerting you before the aspect reaches its apex. As they are eight hours ahead of the Pacific, European countries should consider the day starting at 8:00am. So if the exact aspect perfection occurs before then, the advice will be posted one day before. Most US readers should consider the day to start between 12:00am and 3:00pm as usual. An aspect is always strongest as it builds, and then gradually weakens after it reaches its perfection (same degree and minute). Australian and Asian residents can prepare one day earlier. No matter where you are, with this diary, you will always be ready for the best energy to come!

THE 12 HOUSES OF THE HOROSCOPE

THE FOLLOWING IS THE GENERAL NATURE OF EACH HOUSE:

I. **FIRST HOUSE:** Personality, natural disposition, worldly outlook generally. Physical experiences as obtained through the five senses. The parts of the body denoted are the head and face.

II. **SECOND HOUSE:** Finance, monetary prospects. Self-esteem values, salary, income. Desires caused by the infleunce of the tength house affect moral growth. The parts of the body denoted are the throat and ears.

III. **THIRD HOUSE:** Relatives and kin, travelling, intellect derived from education and study, first education, expression and minor impressions made upon the physical brain. The parts of the body denoted are the neck, arms and shoulders and lungs.

IV. **FOURTH HOUSE:** Hereditary tendencies. Home and domestic life, parentage, ancestry, environment and the general state of things at the close of life. The parts of the body denoted are the breasts, stomach and digestive organs.

V. **FIFTH HOUSE:** Offspring, generative powers, sensations and pleasurable emotions arising from the senses, worldly enterprise and energy. Creativity and talents. The parts of the body denoted are the loins, heart and back.

VI. **SIXTH HOUSE:** Service and attachments arising from the expression of the tenth house; therefore, servants and inferiors in social rank. This house also denotes sickness arising from worry and anxiety. It is also the house of phenomenal magick arising from everyday habits. The parts of the body denoted are the bowels and solar plexus.

VII. **SEVENTH HOUSE:** Union, marriage, partnership, business partner, spouse, individual character and humane tendencies, your client, your other half. The parts of the body denoted are the veins and kidneys.

VIII. **EIGHTH HOUSE:** Death, all matters pertaining to legacies or affairs connected with death. It is also what is termed an occult house. The womb, pregnancy, gestation. Fusion of energies, sexual drive. The parts of the body denoted are the secret parts and the generative system.

IX. **NINTH HOUSE:** Higher mentality, higher studies, scientific, philosophic and religious tendencies. The searching of the path, your truth. It also denotes long journeys, documentation, certificates, dreams and the image-making power. The parts of the body denoted are the thighs and hips.

X. **TENTH HOUSE:** Profession, business ability, fame, honour and material reputation. All worldly activities and moral responsibilities are shown by this house to succeed. The parts of the body denoted are the knees.

XI. **ELEVENTH HOUSE:** Friends, acquaintances, hopes, wishes and aspirations. The groups and environments you belong to. Your audience, your followers. The parts of the body denoted are the legs and ankles.

XII. **TWELFTH HOUSE:** Occult tendencies. Its connection with the fourth house shows the psychic thought inheritance from the past, and the result is either joy or sorrow. This may be said to be the most critical house of the 12. The parts of the body denoted are the feet and toes.

LIFE SATISFACTION CHART

Each section represent an area of your life, or a house in your astral chart.
From a scale of 1 to 10, rate the areas of your chart.
You can use colour pencils to make it artistic!

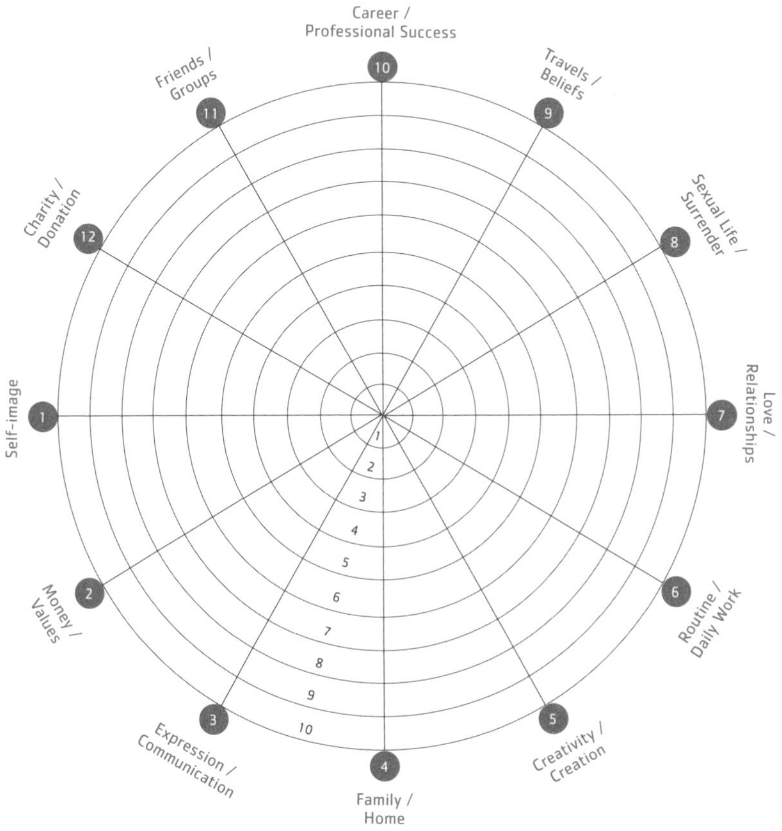

What could you do to increase your level of satisfaction in the areas you have scored the lowest? Which is the area of your life that, when you are satisfied, can improve all the other areas? Take time to think about it, and always come back to this page to track your progress.

SOLSTICES & EQUINOXES NORTH HEMISPHERE

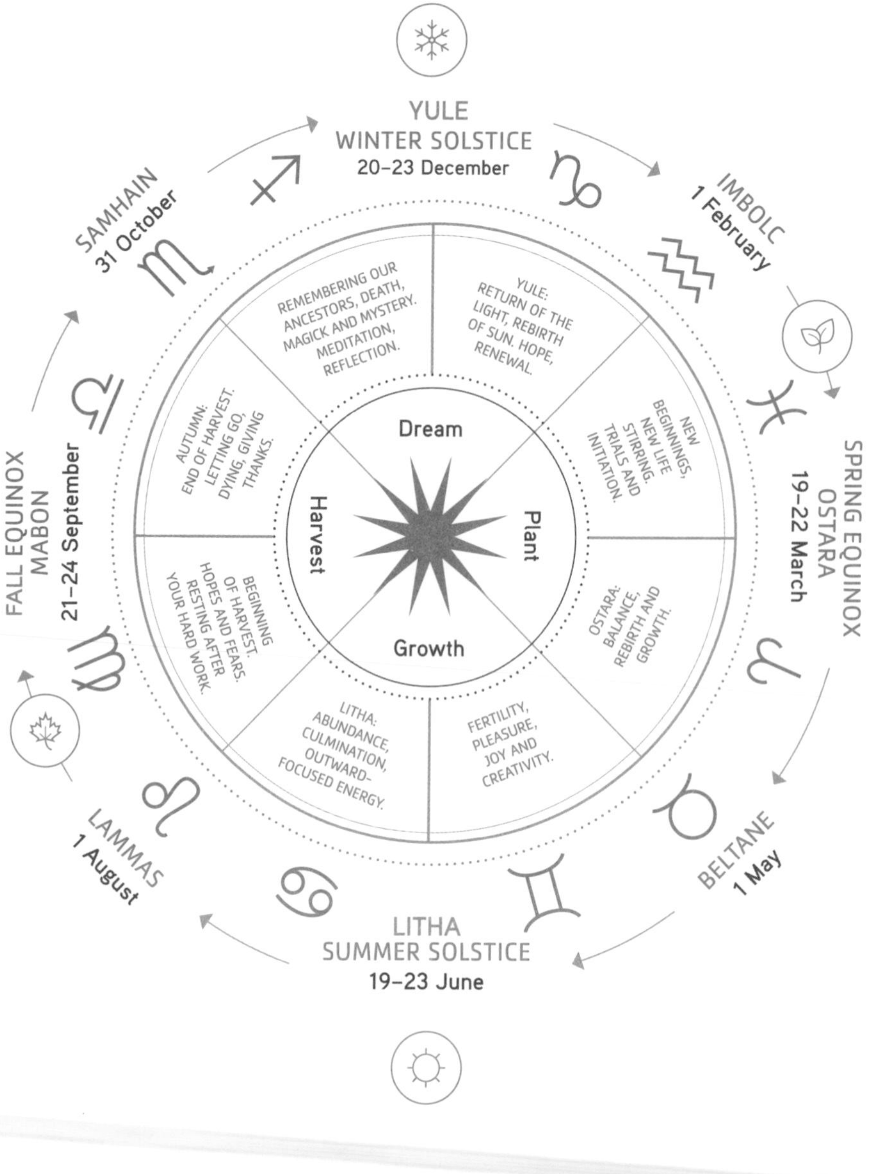

YULE
WINTER SOLSTICE
20–23 December

YULE: RETURN OF THE LIGHT, REBIRTH OF SUN. HOPE, RENEWAL.

IMBOLC
1 February

NEW BEGINNINGS, NEW LIFE STIRRING. TRIALS AND INITIATION.

SPRING EQUINOX
OSTARA
19–22 March

OSTARA: BALANCE, REBIRTH AND GROWTH.

BELTANE
1 May

FERTILITY, PLEASURE, JOY AND CREATIVITY.

LITHA
SUMMER SOLSTICE
19–23 June

LITHA: ABUNDANCE, CULMINATION, OUTWARD-FOCUSED ENERGY.

LAMMAS
1 August

BEGINNING OF HARVEST. HOPES AND FEARS. RESTING AFTER YOUR HARD WORK.

FALL EQUINOX
MABON
21–24 September

AUTUMN: END OF HARVEST. LETTING GO, DYING, GIVING THANKS.

SAMHAIN
31 October

REMEMBERING OUR ANCESTORS, DEATH, MAGICK AND MYSTERY. MEDITATION, REFLECTION.

Dream

Plant

Growth

Harvest

SOLSTICES & EQUINOXES SOUTH HEMISPHERE

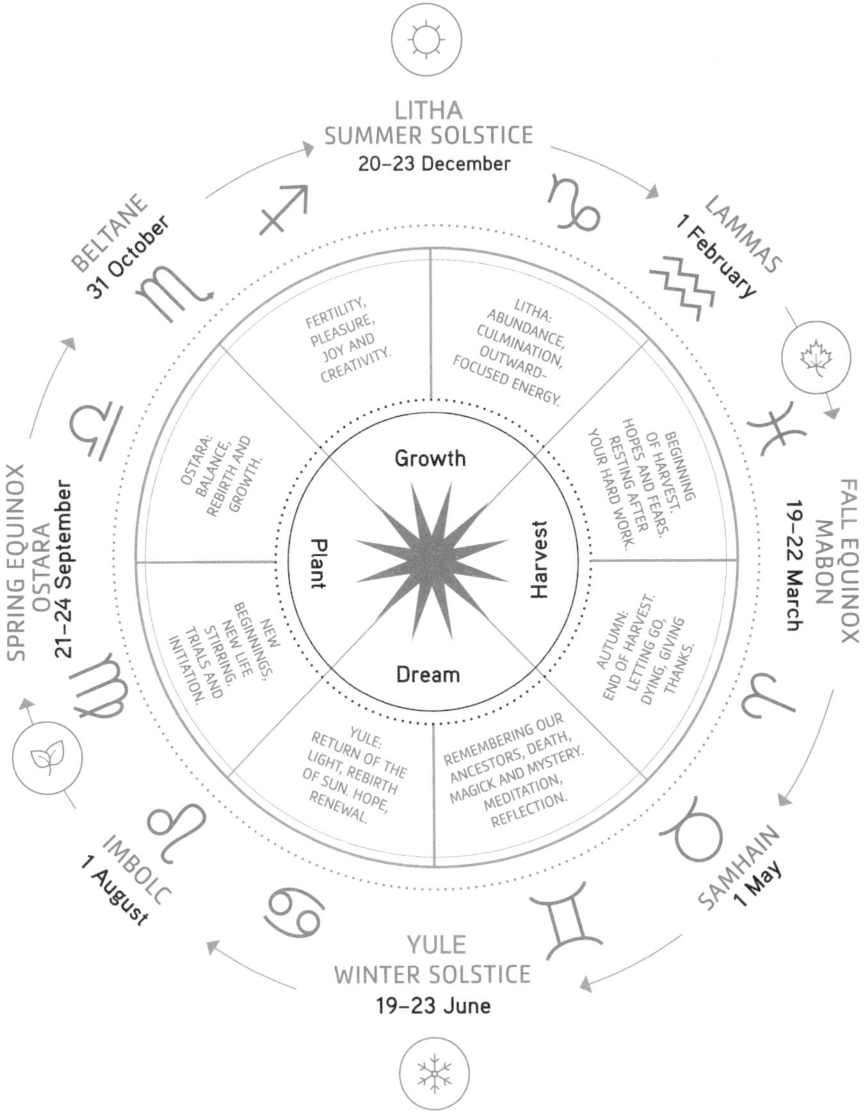

LITHA
SUMMER SOLSTICE
20–23 December

LAMMAS
1 February

FALL EQUINOX
MABON
19–22 March

SAMHAIN
1 May

YULE
WINTER SOLSTICE
19–23 June

IMBOLC
1 August

SPRING EQUINOX
OSTARA
21–24 September

BELTANE
31 October

FERTILITY, PLEASURE, JOY AND CREATIVITY.

LITHA: ABUNDANCE, CULMINATION, OUTWARD-FOCUSED ENERGY.

BEGINNING OF HARVEST. HOPES AND FEARS. RESTING AFTER YOUR HARD WORK.

AUTUMN: END OF HARVEST. LETTING GO, DYING, GIVING THANKS.

REMEMBERING OUR ANCESTORS, DEATH, MAGICK AND MYSTERY. MEDITATION, REFLECTION.

YULE: RETURN OF THE LIGHT, REBIRTH OF SUN. HOPE, RENEWAL.

NEW BEGINNINGS, NEW LIFE STIRRING. TRIALS AND INITIATION.

OSTARA: BALANCE, REBIRTH AND GROWTH.

Growth

Harvest

Dream

Plant

TAROT & ASTROLOGY

MAJOR ARCANA CORRESPONDENCE

Card	Astrology	Meaning
0. THE FOOL	 AIR / URANUS	New beginnings, wonder, innocence, foolishness
1. THE MAGICIAN	 MERCURY	Mastery, creation, willpower, manifestation
2. THE HIGH PRIESTESS	 MOON	Intuition, divine wisdom, inner voice
3. THE EMPRESS	 VENUS	Creativity, beauty, nurturing, fertility
4. THE EMPEROR	 ARIES	Authority, ambition, fostering discipline
5. THE HIEROPHANT	 TAURUS	Tradition, convention, spiritual wisdom
6. THE LOVERS	 GEMINI	Love, union, relationship choices
7. THE CHARIOT	 CANCER	Discipline, self-control, success
8. STRENGTH	 LEO	Courage, inner strength, compassion
9. THE HERMIT	 VIRGO	Insight, awareness, solitude, contemplation
10. WHEEL OF FORTUNE	 JUPITER	Destiny, karma, fate, fortune

11. JUSTICE	 LIBRA	Truth, law, fairness, cause and effect, clarity
12. THE HANGED MAN	 WATER / NEPTUNE	Sacrifice, release, new perspective
13. DEATH	 SCORPIO	Change, transformation, end of cycle
14. TEMPERANCE	 SAGITTARIUS	Patience, finding meaning, balance
15. THE DEVIL	 CAPRICORN	Materialism, pleasure, obsession, addiction
16. THE TOWER	 MARS	Foundational shift, upheaval, drastic change
17. THE STAR	 AQUARIUS	Faith, hope, healing, rejuvenation
18. THE MOON	 PISCES	Intuition, unconsciousness, illusions
19. THE SUN	 SUN	Joy, success, pleasure, celebration
20. JUDGEMENT	 FIRE / PLUTO	Reflection, awakening, reckoning
21. THE WORLD	 EARTH / SATURN	Completion, peace, fulfilment, harmony

A SPELL FOR EACH TIME AND EACH SIGN

COMBINE THE ENERGY OF YOUR SIGN OR THE SIGN IN TRANSIT AT EVERY MOMENT TO IMPROVE YOUR MAGICAL ABILITIES EVEN MORE.

♈	**Fire Witch** – Focuses on the fire element, does a lot of work involving candles, burning, etc.
♉	**Green Witch** – Focused on the use of herbs and plants in magick, very natural and earth-based.
♊	**Crystal Witch** – Works with stones, crystals, gemstones, for healing and other spells, deals with chakras.
♋	**Kitchen Witch** – Uses magick incorporated into cooking and baking. Can conjure items for spells or ritual use.
♌	**Lunar Witch** – Attunes to/honours the Moon cycles and phases. Likes to wake at night under the Moon energy.
♍	**Forest Witch** – Works best surrounded by trees, is familiar with local plants and animals and herbal healing.
♎	**Music Witch** – Its magick is deeply rooted in music, has a certain connection with sound and uses that to enhance rituals.
♏	**Nocturnal Witch** – Embraces darker energies likes night-time and its mysteries. Works mostly after midnight.
♐	**Storm Witch** – Combines its energy with that of the weather. Collects elements such as rainwater, leaves and rocks for spells.
♑	**Astronomy Witch** – All its magick aligns with stars and planets. Practises astrology, recognizes placements and their significances.
♒	**Divination Witch** – Works with various forms of divination, such as tarot reading, palmistry, tea leaves, geomancy.
♓	**Sea Witch** – Uses oceans and their magick practices, utilizing the natural objects in the sea such as salt water, shells, driftwood, etc.

SACRED ALTAR

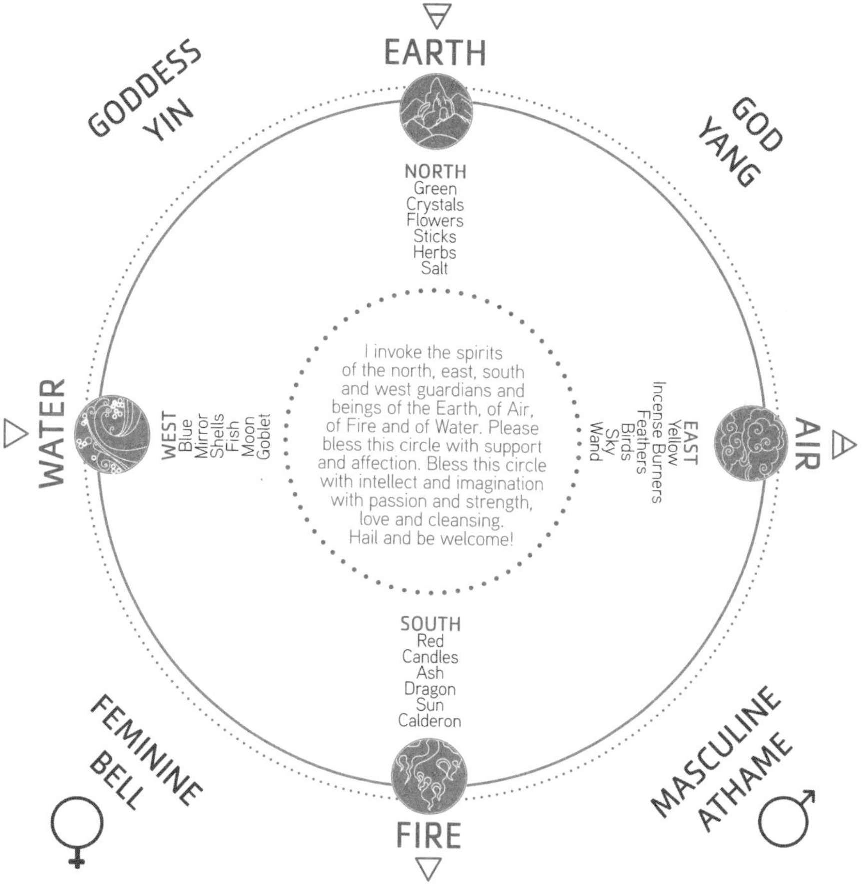

EARTH

GODDESS
YIN

GOD
YANG

NORTH
Green
Crystals
Flowers
Sticks
Herbs
Salt

WATER

WEST
Blue
Mirror
Shells
Fish
Moon
Goblet

I invoke the spirits of the north, east, south and west guardians and beings of the Earth, of Air, of Fire and of Water. Please bless this circle with support and affection. Bless this circle with intellect and imagination with passion and strength, love and cleansing. Hail and be welcome!

EAST
Yellow
Incense Burners
Feathers
Birds
Sky
Wand

AIR

SOUTH
Red
Candles
Ash
Dragon
Sun
Calderon

FEMININE
BELL

FIRE

MASCULINE
ATHAME

A very simple ritual for creating a sacred space is to arrange the elements according to the cardinal directions. The left side has Yin energy, while the right side carries the Yang polarity. Invoke the guardian elements to help you create your own magick. When you have finished your ritual, remember to close the circle, thanking the spirits and saying goodbye to them.

THE DEFINITIVE GUIDE TO SELF-CARE

FOR THE MIND

- Go offline on your social media
- Listen to your favourite music
- Have a bite of something sweet
- Do something creative
- Fix something broken in your house
- Bake a cake or biscuits
- Clean out your wardrobe and donate your clothes
- Watch your favourite film or series
- Take 15 minutes to meditate
- Stain the spaces
- Create a praise pot
- Organize your drawers
- Read a new book
- Prepare a home-cooked meal
- Listen to your favourite podcast
- Drink tea in a nice cup
- Buy yourself some flowers
- Renovate a room in your house
- Organize your desktop files

FOR THE BODY

- Wear your favourite clothes
- Stay outside in the Sun for 15 minutes
- Be still, practise silence
- Light your favourite candle
- Encourage yourself to laugh
- Take a nap if you need to
- Practise breath work
- Run or walk for 30 minutes
- Dance like a child
- Stretch for 20 minutes
- Make a healthier lunch choice
- Take a class, learn something new
- In cold weather, wrap yourself in a soft blanket

FOR THE SOUL

- Help someone
- Write down your thoughts
- Go on a date with yourself
- Listen to your emotions
- Spend time with loved ones
- Play with a pet
- Make up for something you really want
- Reward yourself by practising a hobby
- Hug someone
- Stay home for two days
- Enjoy a home spa
- Call a friend to arrange lunch
- Plan a quick trip to nature
- Spend time alone
- Write a love letter to yourself
- Make a list of things to be grateful for
- Make a visual board with clippings of your future
- Draw a map of all the places you've ever been
- Make a list of dreams
- Cry if you want to
- Go to a bookstore or library
- Look at old photos and videos from the past
- Read poetry
- Make a list of long- and medium-term goals
- Admire yourself in the mirror

2024

JANUARY

M	T	W	T	F	S	S
1	2	3	4	5	**6**	**7**
8	9	10	11	12	**13**	**14**
15	16	17	18	19	**20**	**21**
22	23	24	25	26	**27**	**28**
29	30	31				

FEBRUARY

M	T	W	T	F	S	S
			1	2	**3**	**4**
5	6	7	8	9	**10**	**11**
12	13	14	15	16	**17**	**18**
19	20	21	22	23	**24**	**25**
26	27	28	29			

MARCH

M	T	W	T	F	S	S
				1	**2**	**3**
4	5	6	7	8	**9**	**10**
11	12	13	14	15	**16**	**17**
18	19	20	21	22	**23**	**24**
25	26	27	28	29	**30**	**31**

APRIL

M	T	W	T	F	S	S
1	2	3	4	5	**6**	**7**
8	9	10	11	12	**13**	**14**
15	16	17	18	19	**20**	**21**
22	23	24	25	26	**27**	**28**
29	30					

MAY

M	T	W	T	F	S	S
		1	2	3	**4**	**5**
6	7	8	9	10	**11**	**12**
13	14	15	16	17	**18**	**19**
20	21	22	23	24	**25**	**26**
27	28	29	30	31		

JUNE

M	T	W	T	F	S	S
					1	**2**
3	4	5	6	7	**8**	**9**
10	11	12	13	14	**15**	**16**
17	18	19	20	21	**22**	**23**
24	25	26	27	28	**29**	**30**

JULY

M	T	W	T	F	S	S
1	2	3	4	5	**6**	**7**
8	9	10	11	12	**13**	**14**
15	16	17	18	19	**20**	**21**
22	23	24	25	26	**27**	**28**
29	30	31				

AUGUST

M	T	W	T	F	S	S
			1	2	**3**	**4**
5	6	7	8	9	**10**	**11**
12	13	14	15	16	**17**	**18**
19	20	21	22	23	**24**	**25**
26	27	28	29	30	**31**	

SEPTEMBER

M	T	W	T	F	S	S
						1
2	3	4	5	6	**7**	**8**
9	10	11	12	13	**14**	**15**
16	17	18	19	20	**21**	**22**
23	24	25	26	27	**28**	**29**
30						

OCTOBER

M	T	W	T	F	S	S
	1	2	3	4	**5**	**6**
7	8	9	10	11	**12**	**13**
14	15	16	17	18	**19**	**20**
21	22	23	24	25	**26**	**27**
28	29	30	31			

NOVEMBER

M	T	W	T	F	S	S
				1	**2**	**3**
4	5	6	7	8	**9**	**10**
11	12	13	14	15	**16**	**17**
18	19	20	21	22	**23**	**24**
25	26	27	28	29	**30**	

DECEMBER

M	T	W	T	F	S	S
						1
2	3	4	5	6	**7**	**8**
9	10	11	12	13	**14**	**15**
16	17	18	19	20	**21**	**22**
23	24	25	26	27	**28**	**29**
30	31					

01 JAN NEW YEAR'S DAY
14 FEB VALENTINE'S DAY
20 MAR SPRING EQUINOX
29 MAR GOOD FRIDAY
31 MAR EASTER
01 APR EASTER MONDAY
06 MAY EARLY MAY BANK HOLIDAY (UK)
12 MAY MOTHER'S DAY
27 MAY SPRING BANK HOLIDAY (UK)
18 JUN FATHER'S DAY
21 JUN SUMMER SOLSTICE
26 AUG SUMMER BANK HOLIDAY (UK)
22 SEP AUTUMN EQUINOX
31 OCT HALLOWEEN
28 NOV THANKSGIVING
21 DEC WINTER SOLSTICE
25 DEC CHRISTMAS
31 DEC NEW YEAR'S EVE

JANUARY

the first day
of the month
starts with the
ephemeris

☉	10º	♑
☽	12º	♍
☿℞	22º	♐
♀	3º	♐
♂	27º	♐
♃	5º	♉
♄	3º	♓
♅℞	19º	♉
♆	25º	♓
♇	29º	♑

MON	TUE	WED
01	02	03
08	09	10
15	16	17
22	23	24
29	30	31

THU	FRI	SAT	SUN
04	05	06	07
11	12	13	14
18	19	20	21
25	26	27	28

DEC
31
SUN

♃ D ♉
Jupiter Direct in Taurus

In time for the turning of a new chapter, Jupiter hopes for even more financial and emotional stability. For sure 2024 will be an even more prosperous year and connected with our nature. Happy new cycle!

☽ ♍
Moon in Virgo

JAN
01
MON

♀ ♐ □ ♄ ♓
Venus in Sagittarius squares Saturn in Pisces

At the turn of the year, Venus has her first serious conversation with Saturn, who sets some limits. It could be that you are sacrificing your desires for the sake of something greater. Better that way – save your energy, as the year is just beginning.

☽ ♍
Moon in Virgo

M	T	W	T	F	S	S	M	T	W	T	F	S	S	M	T	W	T	F	S	S	M	T	W	T	F	S	S	M	T	W
1	2	3	4	5	**6**	**7**	8	9	10	11	12	**13**	**14**	15	16	17	18	19	**20**	**21**	22	23	24	25	26	**27**	**28**	29	30	31

JAN
02
TUE

☿ St D ♐
Mercury Stations Direct in 22º Sagittarius

After 20 days, it seems there are pending issues from last year that you view totally differently now. Wait until tomorrow before giving your final word.

☽ ♍
Moon in Virgo

JAN
03
WED

☿ D ♐
Mercury Direct in Sagittarius

Now, with Mercury turned direct, everything that has been waiting for your decision since the second week of December gets the green light. Time to plan your next trips and/or have deep and meaningful conversations. Perhaps you are searching for your new truth. Believe me, you will see the world with fresh eyes this year.

☽ ♎
Moon in Libra

JAN
04
THU

♂ ♑
Mars enters Capricorn until 13 February

This is the aspect we needed to start the year in full force. You want to build your dream future, and this Mars won't waste time; it goes straight to work on whatever has been well planned in advance.

◑ ♎
Last Quarter 13º Libra

On the same day, the Waning Moon warns you that there are certain relationships that may not be letting you reach your maximum potential. Time to let go of any negative beliefs and move on.

JAN
05
FRI

☽ ♏
Moon in Scorpio

M	T	W	T	F	S	S	M	T	W	T	F	S	S	M	T	W	T	F	S	S	M	T	W	T	F	S	S	M	T	W
1	2	3	4	5	6	7	8	9	10	11	12	13	14	15	16	17	18	19	20	21	22	23	24	25	26	27	28	29	30	31

JAN
06
SAT

☽ ♏
Moon in Scorpio

JAN
07
SUN

☽ ♐
Moon in Sagittarius

M	T	W	T	F	S	S	M	T	W	T	F	S	S	M	T	W	T	F	S	S	M	T	W	T	F	S	S	M	T	W
1	2	3	4	5	6	7	8	9	10	11	12	13	14	15	16	17	18	19	20	21	22	23	24	25	26	27	28	29	30	31

JAN
08
MON

☽ ♐
Moon in Sagittarius

JAN
09
TUE

☿ ♐ □ ♆ ♓
Mercury in Sagittarius squares Neptune in Pisces

Daydreaming is what you'd like to do today. If possible, spare some time to think about your next plans, such as how to accomplish that trip you've always dreamed of, or how to prepare for a big presentation. Trust your insights!

☽ ♐
Moon in Sagittarius

M	T	W	T	F	**S**	**S**	M	T	W	T	F	**S**	**S**	M	T	W	T	F	**S**	**S**	M	T	W	T	F	**S**	**S**	M	T	W
1	2	3	4	5	**6**	**7**	8	9	10	11	12	**13**	**14**	15	16	17	18	19	**20**	**21**	22	23	24	25	26	**27**	**28**	29	30	31

צב
ה·ו·י·ה
Meditation for the month of Sh'vat
Scan with your eyes from right to left

C A P R I C O R N

11 JANUARY - 11:57AM (UTC) - NEW MOON 20° CAPRICORN

Los Angeles (UTC −8) • New York (UTC −5) • London (UTC +0)
Paris (UTC +1) • Sydney (UTC +12)

IN THE NEXT SIX MONTHS I WILL MANIFEST...

Security	Long-term goals	Higher state of being
Ambition	Recognition	Merit
Social status	Planning	Reward
Career	Financial stability	Hard work

JAN
10
WED

☉ ♑ △ ♅ ℞ ♉
Sun in Capricorn trine Uranus Retrograde in Taurus

You now not only accept the changes that have got in the way of your plans, but you are totally open to promoting them. For sure, taking your plans in another direction is the best advice today.

♂ ♑ ✶ ♄ ♓
Mars in Capricorn sextile Saturn in Pisces

Although the pace is a little slower right now, you know you are on the right track and, being more attentive, you can even foresee the obstacles. It would be interesting now to learn to delegate a little bit more. Practise patience!

☽ ♑
Moon in Capricorn

JAN
11
THU

New Moon 20º Capricorn

During this New Moon, begin to set your goals and ask yourself how you would like to feel about your work. How do you want to feel in your career this year? More productive? Procrastinating less? Plan your career goals, where you want to go and how you want to feel in 2024.

JAN
12
FRI

♂ ♑ △ ♃ ♉
Mars in Capricorn trine Jupiter in Taurus

An excellent aspect in the heavens, indicating that there are blessings on the way for those who are patient with their own process. Everything you have planted in recent years is beginning to grow in surprising ways. Keep progressing steadily, step by step toward the top of your life.

☽ ♒
Moon in Aquarius

JAN
13
SAT

☿ ♑
Mercury enters Capricorn until 5 February

The right thought at the right time. With Mercury in Capricorn, you gain serious ideas and a penetrating mind. The self-discipline you needed to reprogramme your route to success is here! Take this opportunity to discuss all your greatest ambitions.

☽ ♒
Moon in Aquarius

JAN

14

SUN

☽ ♓

Moon in Pisces

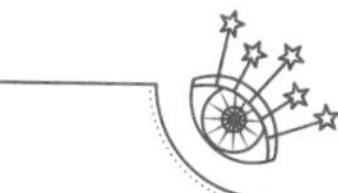

JAN

15

MON

☽ ♓

Moon in Pisces

M	T	W	T	F	S	S	M	T	W	T	F	S	S	M	T	W	T	F	S	S	M	T	W	T	F	S	S	M	T	W
1	2	3	4	5	**6**	**7**	8	9	10	11	12	**13**	**14**	15	16	17	18	19	**20**	**21**	22	23	24	25	26	**27**	**28**	29	30	31

JAN
16
TUE

☉ ♑ ✱ ♆ ♓
Sun in Capricorn sextile Neptune in Pisces

Creativity and intuition make it easier today to create the future you desire. Great day for anything involving the arts, writing and business. Excellent for looking at investments and seeing where you can save money to fund your dreams.

☽ ♈
Moon in Aries

JAN
17
WED

☽ ♈
Moon in Aries

JAN
18
THU

☿ ♑ ⚹ ♄ ♓
Mercury in Capricorn sextile Saturn in Pisces

Bringing the ability to concentrate and a disciplined mind, another excellent aspect that will help you in any studies and research you are involved in. You may feel a bit more methodical and put the right boundaries in place so people don't abuse your goodwill. Focus on the work to be done.

◐ ♈
First Quarter 27º Aries

JAN
19
FRI

☿ ♑ △ ♃ ♉
Mercury in Capricorn trine Jupiter in Taurus

It feels like luck is on your side and today it's easier to visualize what moves should be made now in your life for recognition to come your way. Continue with your positivity by moving forward strategically, but be sure to look at your shortfalls and correct them in the future.

♀ ♐ □ ♆ ♓
Venus in Sagittarius squares Neptune in Pisces

It may be that the difficulty today is dealing with extreme optimism, your exaggerated emotions and the struggle between your intuition and your feelings. Beware of drinking to excess and other medications.

☽ ♉
Moon in Taurus

JAN
20
SAT

☉ ☌ ♇ ♑
Sun meets Pluto in Capricorn

This is the last time the Sun meets Pluto in Capricorn, triggering our deepest desires. Today we are capable of anything! Reflect and write down what your biggest challenges will be in 2024 and how you can overcome them. Think on three levels: physical, mental and spiritual.

☉ ♒
Sun enters Aquarius

The Sun enters Aquarius and we automatically feel more independent. The month starts with us feeling connected to the future, wanting a better world and helping the collective to rise. An excellent moment to cut out unhealthy habits.

☽ ♊
Moon in Gemini

JAN
21
SUN

♇ ♒
Pluto enters Aquarius until 1 September (will retrograde in May)

Sixteen years ago Pluto entered Capricorn for the transit that would bring down the old world. Now he's in Aquarius, we will have just over eight months to determine what he's promising us for the next 19 years. A new humanitarian revolution is beginning to unfold. We will have a fresh idea of what it means to be truly humanitarian soon – wait for it!

☽ ♊
Moon in Gemini

AQUARIUS

20 January / 2:07PM (UTC)

AQUARIUS

MODE Fixed **ELEMENT** Air **RULING PLANET** Uranus

CRYSTAL Cornelian **BACH FLOWER REMEDY** Water Violet

PRINCIPLE Positive **OPPOSIT SIGN** Leo

AQUARIUS AND SIGNS IN LOVE

Aries	♥♥♥♡♡	Libra	♥♥♥♥♥
Taurus	♥♡♡♡♡	Scorpio	♥♥♡♡♡
Gemini	♥♥♥♥♥	Sagittarius	♥♥♥♥♡
Cancer	♥♥♡♡♡	Capricorn	♥♥♡♡♡
Leo	♥♥♥♥♥	Aquarius	♥♥♥♡♡
Virgo	♥♥♡♡♡	Pisces	♥♥♡♡♡

MANTRA I know **POWER** Vision

KEYWORD Imagination **ANATOMY** Ankles

LIGHT
Independent
Inventive
Individualistic
Progressive
Artistic
Logical
Eccentric
Intellectual
Altruistic

SHADOW
Unpredictable
Temperamental
Bored with details
Cold
Stubborn opinions
Shy
Radical
Impersonal
Rebel

JAN
22
MON

☽ ♋
Moon in Cancer

JAN
23
TUE

♀ ♑
Venus enters Capricorn until 16 February

Venus in Capricorn is about the search for financial and emotional stability. This search often hides great insecurity, so it is good to keep an eye out for this. This is a season in which we may neglect our ideals because we have no confidence in our potential. Be true to yourself!

☽ ♋
Moon in Cancer

JAN
24
WED

☽ ♋
Moon in Cancer

JAN
25
THU

○ ♌
Full Moon 5º Leo

Full Moon giving a big boost of joy and sociability. Take a major Aquarian ideal and bring it close to your heart, like when you were a child. Good time to do something artistic or throw a party!

JAN
26
FRI

☽ ♌
Moon in Leo

JAN
27
SAT

☉ ♒ □ ♃ ♉
Sun in Aquarius square Jupiter in Taurus

This Saturday could make you feel quite excited and hopeful. Luck continues to be on your side, but the moment asks you to rein in your ego a little and not risk too much. Blind optimism doesn't suit you, and even luck has its limits.

♅ St D ♉
Uranus Stations Direct 19º in Taurus

After five months of retrogradation, we are ready to give voice to a technological project, or even move forward with our system updates. Anything involving technology gets an even bigger boost.

☿ ☌ ♂ ♑
Mercury meets Mars in Capricorn

When these two meet in the sign of daily work, they bring lots of mental energy and ask you to review your routines and to attend even more closely to what you do. See if you need to slow down your work pace in order to protect your health or if you need to wake up earlier to chase all your dreams.

☽ ♍
Moon in Virgo

JAN
28
SUN

♀ ♑ ✱ ♄ ♓
Venus in Capricorn sextile Saturn in Pisces

A great Sunday for devising a networking strategy. Set your shyness aside and talk more about yourself. Write down in this diary everything you want to express and how you think you'll achieve this.

☿ ♑ △ ♅ ♉
Mercury in Capricorn trine Uranus in Taurus

Revisit your profile on social networks, renew your virtual look, change your photo, refresh copy, delete old comments or give your website a new layout.

♅ D ♉
Uranus Direct in Taurus

With Uranus in direct motion, it's easier to take control of your presence online. Take courses and pick up tips on how to present yourself on the internet to reach the target you are aiming for.

☽ ♍
Moon in Virgo

JAN
29
MON

♀ ♑ △ ♃ ♉
Venus in Capricorn trine Jupiter in Taurus

A Monday that can surprise you with so many blessings! Your popularity may increase, and even yesterday's small actions can start to take effect. Your ability to save money should be in direct proportion to your self-esteem. Be on your guard!

♂ ♑ △ ♅ ♉
Mars in Capricorn trine Uranus in Taurus

Something you have been working hard on, planning it out, may surprise you today. A great time to promote yourself or your company, advertising to reach the right niche. Luck doesn't seem to want to go away, so take advantage of it.

☽ ♍
Moon in Virgo

JAN
30
TUE

☽ ♎
Moon in Libra

JAN
31
WED

☽ ♎
Moon in Libra

M	T	W	T	F	**S**	**S**	M	T	W	T	F	**S**	**S**	M	T	W	T	F	**S**	**S**	M	T	W	T	F	**S**	**S**	M	T	W
1	2	3	4	5	**6**	**7**	8	9	10	11	12	**13**	**14**	15	16	17	18	19	**20**	**21**	22	23	24	25	26	**27**	**28**	29	30	31

FEBRUARY

the first day of the month starts with the ephemeris

☉	12º	♒
☽	25º	♎
☿	24º	♑
♀	11º	♑
♂	21º	♑
♃	7º	♉
♄	6º	♓
♅	19º	♉
♆	26º	♓
♇	0º	♒

MON	TUE	WED
05	06	07
12	13	14
19	20	21
26	27	28

THU	FRI	SAT	SUN
01	02	03	04
08	09	10	11
15	16	17	18
22	23	24	25
29			

FEB
01
THU

☽ ♏
Moon in Scorpio

FEB
02
FRI

☿ ♑ ⚹ ♆ ♓
Mercury in Capricorn sextile Neptune in Pisces

A passionate Friday, you could be starting a love story or falling in love with yourself. Best of all, you're mentally healthy, understanding your processes and not wanting to run away from them. Your self-esteem will vibrate even higher!

◑ ♏
Last Quarter 13º Scorpio

Best Waning Moon of the year for getting rid of low-vibration feelings such as insecurity, jealousy and envy. Prepare a bath with lavender and use a scrub to free yourself from the old shell. Show off your new skin soon!

FEB
03
SAT

☽ ♏
Moon in Scorpio

FEB
04
SUN

☽ ♐
Moon in Sagittarius

FEB
05
MON

☿ ♒
Mercury enters Aquarius until 23 February

We start the week with the greatest excitement, because with Mercury in Aquarius we become more mentally agile. It will be hard to win an argument with you. Great for learning something new!

☿ ☌ ♇ ♒
Mercury meets Pluto in Aquarius

The first conversation of these two planets in Aquarius, and the question is: what have you been wanting to explore lately? Is there an issue requiring your attention or research? A discussion with an important group is also a good idea.

☽ ♐
Moon in Sagittarius

FEB
06
TUE

☽ ♑
Moon in Capricorn

T	F	S	S	M	T	W	T	F	S	S	M	T	W	T	F	S	S	M	T	W	T	F	S	S	M	T	W	T
1	2	**3**	**4**	5	6	7	8	9	**10**	**11**	12	13	14	15	16	**17**	**18**	19	20	21	22	23	**24**	**25**	26	27	28	29

FEB
07
WED

♀ ♑ △ ♅ ♉
Venus in Capricorn trine Uranus in Taurus

Another favourable day to acquire technological goods, or even to take a look at cryptocurrencies. Time to learn a little more about the financial universe that will unfold further in 2024. Seek out the experts!

☽ ♑
Moon in Capricorn

FEB
08
THU

♂ ♑ ✳ ♆ ♓
Mars in Capricorn sextile Neptune in Pisces

Your intuition may have led you to restrict your spending a little, or even sacrifice your personal life, but the effort will be worth it. Rethink your goals and get ready for the New Moon and a weekend among friends. Enjoy!

☉ ♒ □ ♅ ♉
Sun in Aquarius square Uranus in Taurus

A desire to do everything your way can suddenly overwhelm you. This is the time to value your efforts and free yourself from habits and beliefs that limit you, but be careful not to hurt anyone with your honesty today.

☽ ♒
Moon in Aquarius

FEB
09
FRI

● ♒
New Moon 20º Aquarius

Time to define your intentions toward the groups and friends in your life. How can you add even more value to your community? How would you like to receive support from your friends? What is your vision of an ideal world? Reflect on this, and take the opportunity to join your fellows.

FEB
10
SAT

☿ ♒ □ ♃ ♉
Mercury in Aquarius squares Jupiter in Taurus

Another Saturday ahead of the curve, leaving you wanting to overdo everything, especially the rules you impose on yourself. There are no shortcuts to long-lasting success; you must learn to climb step by step without trying to bluff your way up the ladder. That is your mission today.

☽ ♓
Moon in Pisces

קג
ה·ה·י·ו
Meditation for the month of Adar I
Scan with your eyes from right to left

A Q U A R I U S

9 FEBRUARY – 10:59PM (UTC) – NEW MOON 20° AQUARIUS

Los Angeles (UTC –8) • New York (UTC –5) • London (UTC +0)
Paris (UTC +1) • Sydney (UTC +12)

IN THE NEXT SIX MONTHS I WILL MANIFEST...

New friendships
Collectivity
New projects
Innovation

The future
Internet and social
Networks
Eccentricity

Detachment
Leaving addictions
Originality
Activism

FEB
11
SUN

☽ ♓
Moon in Pisces

FEB
12
MON

☽ ♈
Moon in Aries

T	F	**S**	**S**	M	T	W	T	F	**S**	**S**	M	T	W	T	F	**S**	**S**	M	T	W	T	F	**S**	**S**	M	T	W	T
1	2	**3**	**4**	5	6	7	8	9	**10**	**11**	12	13	14	15	16	**17**	**18**	19	20	21	22	23	**24**	**25**	26	27	28	29

FEB
13
TUE

♂ ♒
Mars enters Aquarius until 22 March

We will feel strategically minded during this transit. Our ideals gain a boost, and we can sense the rewards arriving from far away; our vision is amplified and becomes more modern. Great for leading groups, forming a team and being in charge; just be careful not to try to overthrow the established order and put everything at risk.

♀ ♑ ⚹ ♆ ♓
Venus in Capricorn sextile Neptune in Pisces

A super-romantic outlook on the eve of Valentine's Day. Take advantage of your charm to win the heart of the one you love the most! Live a love story, the kind that makes you want to build an empire with your loved one. Love yourself even more today.

☽ ♈
Moon in Aries

FEB
14
WED

♂ ☌ ♇ ♒
Mars meets Pluto in Aquarius

In this, their first conversation in Aquarius, Pluto calls Mars into a corner to focus on all the innovations he wants to implement in the sign of the water-bearer. Develop your courage and drive, without getting too obsessed over a particular idea.

☽ ♉
Moon in Taurus

FEB
15
THU

☽ ♉
Moon in Taurus

FEB
16
FRI

♀ ♒
Venus enters Aquarius until 11 March

Now it's Venus's turn: maybe you gain a more modern and liberal look, and want to experiment a little more with your freedom. A Friday to be guided by your own rules, in life and in love!

First Quarter 27º Taurus

The Waxing Crescent Moon helping you to grow the intentions of the New Moon in Aquarius. Be persistent in not falling back into old habits, visualize your life the way you would like it to be, and don't take your focus off that image until it becomes reality.

FEB
17
SAT

☿ ♒ □ ♅ ♉
Mercury in Aquarius squares Uranus in Taurus

An eccentric Saturday, making you inclined not to follow rules or listen to advice. Channel all that energy into science, philosophy, politics or writing, and be very careful that your boldness doesn't seem arrogant.

♀ ☌ ♇ ♒
Venus meets Pluto in Aquarius

After her time with Mars, Venus discusses with Pluto how to be more liberated in relationships, and how to let go of old and outdated societal norms and live in abundance. Pluto wants everyone to have their wishes fulfilled and promises to let everyone follow their own rules for happiness.

☽ ♊
Moon in Gemini

FEB
18
SUN

☽ ♊
Moon in Gemini

PISCES

19 February / 4:13AM (UTC)

PISCES

MODE Mutable **ELEMENT** Water **RULING PLANET** Neptune

CRYSTAL Amethyst **BACH FLOWER REMEDY** Rock Rose

PRINCIPLE Negative **OPPOSITE SIGN** Virgo

PISCES AND SIGNS IN LOVE

Aries	♥ ♥ ♥ ♡ ♡	Libra	♥ ♥ ♡ ♡ ♡
Taurus	♥ ♥ ♥ ♥ ♡	Scorpio	♥ ♥ ♥ ♥ ♥
Gemini	♥ ♡ ♡ ♡ ♡	Sagittarius	♥ ♥ ♥ ♥ ♡
Cancer	♥ ♥ ♥ ♡ ♡	Capricorn	♥ ♥ ♥ ♡ ♡
Leo	♥ ♥ ♥ ♥ ♡	Aquarius	♥ ♥ ♡ ♡ ♡
Virgo	♥ ♥ ♥ ♥ ♥	Pisces	♥ ♥ ♥ ♥ ♥

MANTRA I Believe **POWER** Comprehension

KEYWORD Intuition **ANATOMY** Feet

LIGHT
Compassionate
Charitable
Friendly
Emotional
Makes sacrifices
Intuitive
Introspective
Musical
Artistic

SHADOW
Procrastinator
Very talkative
Melancholic
Pessimistic
Emotionally inhibited
Shy
Not practical
Indolent
Often feels misunderstood

FEB
19
MON

☉ ♓
Sun enters Pisces

We begin the most mystical month of the year: with the Sun entering Pisces, everyone can dream even higher. With this sign's spirit of sacrifice, in the next 30 days we will become more altruistic and artistic. Good for all work that involves art and helping others.

☽ ♋
Moon in Cancer

FEB
20
TUE

☽ ♋
Moon in Cancer

FEB
21
WED

☽ ♌
Moon in Leo

FEB
22
THU

♀ ☌ ♂ ♒
Venus meets Mars in 7º Aquarius

Love, companionship and open relations are greatly benefited by this meeting of the cosmic couple in the sky. You may also be inviting new people into your life and into your particular universe. Just save your financial resources a little bit more for these days.

☽ ♌
Moon in Leo

FEB
23
FRI

☿ ♓
Mercury enters Pisces until 10 March

After a very dynamic season, Mercury enters Pisces and becomes more sensorial. All forms of artistic expression gain even more visibility. Time to donate a little to those in need.

☽ ♌
Moon in Leo

FEB
24
SAT

○ ♍
Full Moon 5º Virgo

Perfect Saturday for a big creative party. This Full Moon consecrates the self-expression of your spiritual and intuitive journey. Look at your entire past year and consider where you can grow further. Practise journaling and meditation until the next New Moon.

FEB
25
SUN

♀ ♒ □ ♃ ♉
Venus in Aquarius squares Jupiter in Taurus

Now it's Venus who observes whether you've been a little too exaggerated and self-indulgent lately. This aspect indicates excessive vanity and a desire to use people as it suits you. Be careful, as they may do the same to you.

☽ ♍
Moon in Virgo

FEB
26
MON

☽ ♎
Moon in Libra

FEB
27
TUE

♂ ♒ □ ♃ ♉
Mars in Aquarius squares Jupiter in Taurus

It's Mars's turn to aspect Jupiter, which reminds you to develop the self-discipline and awareness needed to achieve the highest levels. Perhaps you are wasting your talent in a job that rewards your pocket but not your soul? Think about it.

☽ ♎
Moon in Libra

FEB
28
WED

☉ ☌ ☿ ☌ ♄ ♓
Sun meets Mercury and Saturn in Pisces

A triple conjunction, announcing that it is time to live your dreams and not allow any person to diminish your light. Learning to establish boundaries is the first step to strengthening the individuality that you deserve this year.

☽ ♎
Moon in Libra

FEB
29
THU

☿ ♓ ✱ ♃ ♉
Mercury in Pisces sextile Jupiter in Taurus

A great Thursday for indulging your senses, listening to good music or giving yourself a nice massage. This aspect also stimulates creativity, so you can express yourself in any way you like. Meditation to the sound of Tibetan bowls can inspire you even more.

☽ ♏
Moon in Scorpio

MARCH

the first day of the month starts with the ephemeris

☉	11º	♓
☽	16º	♏
☿	12º	♓
♀	17º	♒
♂	13º	♒
♃	11º	♉
♄	10º	♓
♅	20º	♉
♆	27º	♓
♇	1º	♒

MON	TUE	WED
04	05	06
11	12	13
18	19	20
25	26	27

THU	FRI	SAT	SUN
	01	02	03
07	08	09	10
14	15	16	17
21	22	23	24
28	29	30	31

MAR
01
FRI

☉ ♓ ⚹ ♃ ♉
Sun in Pisces sextile Jupiter in Taurus

A lazy and indulgent Friday. You know how to treat yourself and today is a good day for that. Take care of both yourself and your finances – you may be spending what you haven't received yet. Talk about your feelings with someone who values you.

☽ ♏
Moon in Scorpio

MAR
02
SAT

☽ ♐
Moon in Sagittarius

MAR
03
SUN

♀ ♒ □ ♅ ♉

Venus in Aquarius squares Uranus in Taurus

This Sunday may be surprising because you could realize that you are doing everything your own way, without expecting or needing others in your life. This may be a very good thing, but perhaps it takes you away from deeper connections, and makes you appear cold and distant. Try to balance your independence with quality time with the ones you love.

Last Quarter 13º Sagittarius

Let go of the part of yourself that puts you in a selfish position and which believes that only you know how to do things the way you do. This disconnects you from your spirituality, which knows that we are all one. Get inspired and dispense with ways of seeing the world that are no longer appropriate.

MAR
04
MON

☿ ♓ ✶ ♅ ♉

Mercury in Pisces sextile Uranus in Taurus

This week you can transform the way you monetize your talents. Today's planetary chat inspires you to talk to someone important, releasing your talents. Seek out an expert in your field.

☽ ♑

Moon in Capricorn

F	**S**	**S**	M	T	W	T	F	**S**	**S**	M	T	W	T	F	**S**	**S**	M	T	W	T	F	**S**	**S**	M	T	W	T	F	**S**	**S**
1	**2**	**3**	4	5	6	7	8	**9**	**10**	11	12	13	14	15	**16**	**17**	18	19	20	21	22	**23**	**24**	25	26	27	28	29	**30**	**31**

MAR
05
TUE

☽ ♑
Moon in Capricorn

MAR
06
WED

☽ ♑
Moon in Capricorn

F	S	S	M	T	W	T	F	S	S	M	T	W	T	F	S	S	M	T	W	T	F	S	S	M	T	W	T	F	S	S
1	**2**	**3**	4	5	6	7	8	**9**	**10**	11	12	13	14	15	**16**	**17**	18	19	20	21	22	**23**	**24**	25	26	27	28	29	**30**	**31**

MAR
07
THU

☽ ♒
Moon in Aquarius

MAR
08
FRI

☿ ☌ ♆ ♓
Mercury meets Neptune in Pisces

It makes for a most romantic Friday when these two meet in the sky. Good for enjoying literature, writing, music, poetry, films and shows. Invite your partner to enjoy an evening of conversation and fantasy. Board games are also welcome, but leave competitiveness aside.

☽ ♒
Moon in Aquarius

MAR
09
SAT

♂ ♒ □ ♅ ♉
Mars in Aquarius squares Uranus in Taurus

Learn to control your temper and you will go far. This aspect makes us very inattentive, which may cause an accident. Be careful to choose the right words and not contradict yourself.

☉ ♓ ✱ ♅ ♉
Sun in Pisces sextile Uranus in Taurus

Your leadership skills attract a lot of attention. You could get involved in a cause or social movement and be very successful – just watch your emotions so you don't get them mixed up with those of others. Move forward in life like this.

☽ ♓
Moon in Pisces

MAR
10
SUN

☿ ♈
Mercury enters Aries until 15 May (will retrograde)

This year Mercury retrogrades in the Fire signs, bringing even more divine inspiration into our lives. It'd be wonderful to learn how to improvise and be a little impulsive. Do not focus on tasks that demand too much concentration, because there will be a tendency to change your point of view from one moment to the next.

☿ ♈ ✱ ♇ ♒
Mercury in Aries sextile Pluto in Aquarius

Already close to Pluto, this aspect releases the urge to be the first in everything, and to do things your own way. If well channelled, today's energy can lead you to win praise for your acts in relation to the collective.

● ♓
New Moon 20º Pisces

The New Moon arrives to fuel our dreams and inspire us to dream higher. Tonight, set your intentions on how to work with your intuition and inner awareness this year. Can you find more powerful ways to stay in a meditative state, connecting with your intuition and creativity?

קג
ה·ה·י·ו
Meditation for the month of Adar II
Scan with your eyes from right to left

P I S C E S

10 MARCH - 9:00AM (UTC) - NEW MOON 20° PISCES

Los Angeles (UTC −7) • New York (UTC −4) • London (UTC +0)
Paris (UTC +1) • Sydney (UTC +11)

IN THE NEXT SIX MONTHS I WILL MANIFEST...

Inspiration Unconditional love Enlightenment Mysticism	Transcendence Compassion Spirituality Collective unconscious	Intuition Altruism Philanthropy Charity

MAR
11
MON

♀ ♓
Venus enters Pisces until 5 April

An extremely compassionate energy. Venus in Pisces is mystical and artistic, and has a spirituality that overflows. Ruled by love, she pursues her fantasies but often lacks a little realism and forethought. Put the focus on your talents, but check whether you are becoming overdependent on the emotions of others to validate yourself.

☽ ♈
Moon in Aries

MAR
12
TUE

☽ ♈
Moon in Aries

MAR
13
WED

☽ ♉
Moon in Taurus

MAR
14
THU

☽ ♉
Moon in Taurus

MAR
15
FRI

☽ ♊
Moon in Gemini

MAR
16
SAT

☽ ♊
Moon in Gemini

MAR
17
SUN

☉ ☌ ♆ ♓
Sun meets Neptune in Pisces

A sensitive Sunday, with Neptune attracting the Sun's full attention to you! Get together with your people and dance, be happy and create memories. It's that kind of memorable Sunday.

◐ ♊
First Quarter 27º Gemini

Take advantage of the Crescent Moon and create something with friends, be it a date or an activity, virtual or, better yet, live and in person. Have fun and feel like you haven't felt in a long time.

MAR
18
MON

☽ ♋
Moon in Cancer

ARIES

20 March / 3:06AM (UTC)

ARIES

MODE Cardinal **ELEMENT** Fire **RULING PLANET** Mars

CRYSTAL Pyrite **BACH FLOWER REMEDY** Impatiens

PRINCIPLE Positive **OPPOSITE SIGN** Libra

ARIES AND SIGNS IN LOVE

Aries	♥ ♥ ♥ ♡ ♡	Libra	♥ ♥ ♥ ♥ ♥
Taurus	♥ ♡ ♡ ♡ ♡	Scorpio	♥ ♥ ♡ ♡ ♡
Gemini	♥ ♥ ♥ ♥ ♥	Sagittarius	♥ ♥ ♥ ♥ ♡
Cancer	♥ ♥ ♡ ♡ ♡	Capricorn	♥ ♥ ♡ ♡ ♡
Leo	♥ ♥ ♥ ♥ ♡	Aquarius	♥ ♥ ♥ ♡ ♡
Virgo	♥ ♥ ♡ ♡ ♡	Pisces	♥ ♥ ♡ ♡ ♡

MANTRA I am **POWER** Action

KEYWORD Assert **ANATOMY** Head, Face, Brain

LIGHT
Pioneer
Competitive
Executive
Impulsive
Courageous
Independent
Dynamic
Living in the present
Fast

SHADOW
Dominator
Irascible
Violent
Intolerant
Rushed
Arrogant
"Me first"
Rude
Has no persistence

MAR
19
TUE

☽ ♌
Moon in Leo

MAR
20
WED

☉ ♈
Sun enters Aries

The Sun crosses the 0th degree of the sign of Aries, and we embark on another turn around the Zodiac. A new time is coming and this is a great period in which to take the initiative and start new things. What will you discover this year?

Fall Equinox - Ostara North Hemisphere
Spring Equinox - Mabon South Hemisphere

☽ ♌
Moon in Leo

MAR
21
THU

☉ ♈ ⚹ ♇ ♒
Sun in Aries sextile Pluto in Aquarius

The first conversation of the Sun in Aries with Pluto asks you to enhance your skills and develop your talents to make a difference this year and leave your mark. We are living through major world transformations, and we need to be wholeheartedly engaged in the process. Be conscious of your work here on Earth.

♀ ☌ ♄ ♓
Venus meets Saturn in Pisces

The Venus that started out all passionate in Pisces is now learning to impose limits on the people she loves. Excellent time to show how emotionally mature you are. Keep up the inner work!

☽ ♌
Moon in Leo

MAR
22
FRI

♂ ♓
Mars enters Pisces until 30 April

To enjoy the weekend, Mars dives into Pisces and you feel like partying! Enjoy the extended season of daydreaming and fulfil your fantasies in life and in love.

☽ ♍
Moon in Virgo

MAR
23
SAT

☽ ♍
Moon in Virgo

MAR
24
SUN

♀ ♓ ⚹ ♃ ♉
Venus in Pisces sextile Jupiter in Taurus

The conversation with Saturn has matured the emotions of this Venus, who now only wants to be esteemed. A good moment to evaluate how appreciated you feel in relation to last year. Keep evolving!

☽ ♎
Moon in Libra

MAR
25
MON

○ ♎
Full Moon Penumbral Eclipse 5º Libra

We start the week vibrating with equality in relationships with this Eclipse. We are all beings in need of love, and relationships help us to understand each other as inhabitants of the same planet. Celebrate the delight of being able to love without limits – as we do so, we can learn so much about ourselves through each other! This Eclipse can change everything in your love relationships, take the opportunity to uplift yourself!

MAR
26
TUE

☽ ♎
Moon in Libra

MAR
27
WED

☽ ♏
Moon in Scorpio

MAR
28
THU

♀ ♓ ✱ ♅ ♉
Venus in Pisces sextile Uranus in Taurus

The response to your efforts comes in the form of compliments on social networks. Good time to talk about self-esteem or get a boost to celebrate yours. You deserve to be in a surprisingly cherished place.

☽ ♏
Moon in Scorpio

MAR
29
FRI

☽ ♐
Moon in Sagittarius

MAR
30
SAT

☽ ♐
Moon in Sagittarius

MM
31
SUN

☽ ♐
Moon in Sagittarius

F	**S**	**S**	M	T	W	T	F	**S**	**S**	M	T	W	T	F	**S**	**S**	M	T	W	T	F	**S**	**S**	M	T	W	T	F	**S**	**S**
1	**2**	**3**	4	5	6	7	8	**9**	**10**	11	12	13	14	15	**16**	**17**	18	19	20	21	22	**23**	**24**	25	26	27	28	29	**30**	**31**

APR IL

the first day of the month starts with the ephemeris

☉	12º	♈
☽	4º	♑
☿	27º	♈
♀	25º	♓
♂	7º	♓
♃	17º	♉
♄	14º	♓
♅	21º	♉
♆	28º	♓
♇	1º	♒

MON	TUE	WED
01	02	03
08	09	10
15	16	17
22	23	24
29	30	

THU	FRI	SAT	SUN
04	05	06	07
11	12	13	14
18	19	20	21
25	26	27	28

APR
01
MON

☿ St ℞ ♈
Mercury Stations Retrograde in 27º Aries

It may seem like a joke, but it's Mercury getting in our way this Monday. Beware of the pranks of this naughty planet. We'll have 24 days to work on our patience with each other. Let's try to make progress!

☽ ♑
Moon in Capricorn

APR
02
TUE

☿ ℞ ♈
Mercury Retrograde in Aries until 25 April

Count to ten when you think that someone is taking up too much of your time, patience and tolerance. The tendency to debate and to be sarcastic could end up putting everything at risk. Take a deep breath this month.

◑ ♑
Last Quarter 12º Capricorn

A deep spring clean is what you need to let go of any emotion, belief, agreement or relationship that is holding you back from vibrating with total confidence. Be practical about saying goodbye.

APR
03
WED

♀ ☌ ♆ ♓
Venus meets Neptune in Pisces

After letting go of a pretty challenging emotional burden, you deserve to reward yourself – and this day is quite romantic if you know how to enjoy it. From the moment you wake up, observe your inner dialogue and only allow yourself to give compliments; leave complaints for another time. Listen to classical music and calm your nerves!

☽ ♒
Moon in Aquarius

APR
04
THU

☽ ♒
Moon in Aquarius

APR
05
FRI

♀ ♈
Venus enters Aries until 29 April

After all the major lessons in self-esteem, Venus is now preparing for a very spicy season. Embarrassment is gone for a while and you're feeling more fearless. Take this opportunity to go where you wouldn't have had the courage to go before, physically and metaphorically.

☽ ♓
Moon in Pisces

APR
06
SAT

♀ ♈ ✶ ♇ ♒
Venus in Aries sextile Pluto in Aquarius

Pluto guarantees Venus at the outset that if she keeps her independent but helpful stance, she will reach even more interesting positions. The Eclipse approaches and an old identity says goodbye to you now.

☽ ♓
Moon in Pisces

ה ד
י·ה·ו·ה
Meditation for the month of Nissan
Scan with your eyes from right to left

A R I E S

8 APRIL - 6:21PM (UTC) - NEW MOON 19° ARIES TOTAL ECLIPSE

Los Angeles (UTC −7) • New York (UTC −4) • London (UTC +1) • Paris (UTC +2) • Sydney (UTC +11)

IN THE NEXT SIX MONTHS I WILL MANIFEST...

New cycle
Energy of beginnings
Impulse
Strength and courage

Passion
New image
Initiative and proactivity
Leadership

Acceptance of risks
Self-challenge
New developments
Physical training

APR
07
SUN

☽ ♈
Moon in Aries

APR
08
MON

● ♈
New Moon Total Eclipse 19º Aries

Let go of an outdated way of thinking about yourself as a human and as a citizen of this world. Time to be a little selfish and focus on realizing your biggest goals, now that everything is starting to change. Look at your priorities first and think about where you want to go and why. Renew your confidence in yourself and you'll make the right choice.

APR
09
TUE

☽ ♉
Moon in Taurus

APR
10
WED

♂ ☌ ♄ ♓
Mars meets Saturn in Pisces

After the Eclipse, now it's Mars who wants us to learn not to get so mixed up in others, but to have a compassionate heart while separating our emotions from our good intentions. It is time to appreciate the value of your time and talent, and no longer underestimate yourself.

☽ ♉
Moon in Taurus

APR
11
THU

☉ ☌ ☿ ℞ ♈
Sun meets Mercury Retrograde in Aries

At the midpoint of the retrogradation, it's time to glimpse your new personality, reborn from within yourself after the Eclipse. Time to make yourself a higher priority in your own life.

☽ ♊
Moon in Gemini

APR
12
FRI

☽ ♊
Moon in Gemini

APR
13
SAT

☽ ♋
Moon in Cancer

APR
14
SUN

☽ ♋
Moon in Cancer

APR
15
MON

◐ ♋
First Quarter 26º Cancer

Choose to please yourself, to nurture yourself. Treat yourself with all the care you would show a baby. When you build your inner confidence, you learn to nurture yourself. Listen to the dark corners of your soul and turn on your light.

APR
16
TUE

☽ ♌
Moon in Leo

M	T	W	T	F	S	S	M	T	W	T	F	S	S	M	T	W	T	F	S	S	M	T	W	T	F	S	S	M	T
1	2	3	4	5	**6**	**7**	8	9	10	11	12	**13**	**14**	15	16	17	18	19	**20**	**21**	22	23	24	25	26	**27**	**28**	29	30

APR
17
WED

☽ ♌
Moon in Leo

APR
18
THU

☽ ♍
Moon in Virgo

TAURUS

19 April / 2:00PM (UTC)

TAURUS

MODE Fixed **ELEMENT** Earth **RULING PLANET** Venus

CRYSTAL Emerald **BACH FLOWER REMEDY** Gentian

PRINCIPLE Negative **OPPOSITE SIGN** Scorpio

TAURUS AND SIGNS IN LOVE

Aries	♥ ♡ ♡ ♡ ♡	Libra	♥ ♥ ♥ ♥ ♡
Taurus	♥ ♥ ♥ ♥ ♡	Scorpio	♥ ♥ ♥ ♥ ♥
Gemini	♥ ♥ ♡ ♡ ♡	Sagittarius	♥ ♡ ♡ ♡ ♡
Cancer	♥ ♥ ♥ ♡ ♡	Capricorn	♥ ♥ ♥ ♡ ♡
Leo	♥ ♥ ♥ ♥ ♡	Aquarius	♥ ♥ ♡ ♡ ♡
Virgo	♥ ♥ ♥ ♥ ♥	Pisces	♥ ♥ ♥ ♥ ♡

MANTRA I have **POWER** Stability

KEYWORD Possess **ANATOMY** Neck, Ears, Vocal cords, Thyroid, Tongue, Throat, Mouth, Tonsils

LIGHT

Patient
Conservative
Sensual
Scrupulous
Stable
Trustworthy
Practical
Loyal

SHADOW

Self-indulgent
Stubborn
Slow
Prone to discussion
Irascible
Possessive
Gluttonous
Materialist

APR
19
FRI

☿ ℞ ☌ ♀ ♈
Mercury Retrograde meets Venus in Aries

Mercury finds his best friend, who helps him formulate his thoughts before he explodes.

♂ ♓ ✱ ♃ ♉
Mars in Pisces sextile Jupiter in Taurus

Mars has a conversation with Jupiter and Uranus, promising to move toward the recognition you've been waiting for, for so long. It's quite possible that this new self-esteem will make you dream even bigger.

♂ ♓ ✱ ♅ ♉
Mars in Pisces sextile Uranus in Taurus

Anything can happen, and now that you feel you can, anything is possible. Create a miracle in your life!

☉ ♉
Sun enters Taurus

After so many discoveries and surprises, the Sun enters Taurus to ground everything we are feeling in this intense season. Take off your shoes and feel the grass touching your feet.

☽ ♍
Moon in Virgo

APR
20
SAT

☽ ♍
Moon in Virgo

M	T	W	T	F	**S**	**S**	M	T	W	T	F	**S**	**S**	M	T	W	T	F	**S**	**S**	M	T	W	T	F	**S**	**S**	M	T
1	2	3	4	5	**6**	**7**	8	9	10	11	12	**13**	**14**	15	16	17	18	19	**20**	**21**	22	23	24	25	26	**27**	**28**	29	30

APR
21
SUN

♃ ☌ ♅ ♉
Jupiter meets Uranus in Taurus

A meeting of the giants this Sunday that is not very peaceful. The time has come to work on your finances and learn about investments. You have many assets, which, with your self-esteem in good order, will make you worth more and more.

☉ ♉ □ ♇ ♒
Sun in Taurus squares Pluto in Aquarius

Pluto pulls the Sun aside and says that your relationship with money needs a fresh look. A powerful time to learn more about investments and digital cryptocurrencies.

☽ ♎
Moon in Libra

APR
22
MON

☽ ♎
Moon in Libra

M	T	W	T	F	S	S	M	T	W	T	F	S	S	M	T	W	T	F	S	S	M	T	W	T	F	S	S	M	T
1	2	3	4	5	**6**	**7**	8	9	10	11	12	**13**	**14**	15	16	17	18	19	**20**	**21**	22	23	24	25	26	**27**	**28**	29	30

APR
23
TUE

○ ♏
Full Moon 4º Scorpio

A perceptive Full Moon, helping you to bring to light all those insecurities that insist on remaining hidden even from yourself. This Full Moon, you celebrate the greatest transformation you have ever experienced in your Life. Welcome to the new you!

APR
24
WED

☽ ♏
Moon in Scorpio

M	T	W	T	F	S	S	M	T	W	T	F	S	S	M	T	W	T	F	S	S	M	T	W	T	F	S	S	M	T
1	2	3	4	5	**6**	**7**	8	9	10	11	12	**13**	**14**	15	16	17	18	19	**20**	**21**	22	23	24	25	26	**27**	**28**	29	30

APR
25
THU

☿ St D ♈
Mercury Stations Direct in 15º Aries

Without further delay, Mercury is already hurrying to end this retrograde movement. We have learned many lessons and we have had to face many anxieties, but it was worth it! Time to breathe more calmly.

☽ ♏
Moon in Scorpio

APR
26
FRI

☿ D ♈
Mercury Direct in Aries

A perfect Friday to have fun, improvise, watch a comedy or go see a stand-up. Look for opportunities to have fun and laugh a lot in the company of friends. Socialize!

☽ ♐
Moon in Sagittarius

M	T	W	T	F	**S**	**S**	M	T	W	T	F	**S**	**S**	M	T	W	T	F	**S**	**S**	M	T	W	T	F	**S**	**S**	M	T
1	2	3	4	5	**6**	**7**	8	9	10	11	12	**13**	**14**	15	16	17	18	19	**20**	**21**	22	23	24	25	26	**27**	**28**	29	30

APR
27
SAT

☽ ♐
Moon in Sagittarius

APR
28
SUN

☽ ♑
Moon in Capricorn

M	T	W	T	F	**S**	**S**	M	T	W	T	F	**S**	**S**	M	T	W	T	F	**S**	**S**	M	T	W	T	F	**S**	**S**	M	T
1	2	3	4	5	**6**	**7**	8	9	10	11	12	**13**	**14**	15	16	17	18	19	**20**	**21**	22	23	24	25	26	**27**	**28**	29	30

APR
29
MON

♂ ☌ ♆ ♓
Mars meets Neptune in Pisces

A scattered and lazy Monday, you may lack energy for the most important things, so try not to schedule anything too complex or demanding today. Relax and take care of yourself!

♀ ♉
Venus enters Taurus until 23 May

Another reason to treat yourself to a coffee in bed, a brunch or even an afternoon tea with friends that could turn into drinks and dinner. If you buy flowers, arrange a beautiful vase in your favourite spot.

☽ ♑
Moon in Capricorn

APR
30
TUE

♂ ♈
Mars enters Aries until 9 June

Tuesday is the best day of the week to take action, and with Mars entering one of his houses, it's like lighting the fire with a rocket! This energy will make the time go faster, so enjoy the ride.

☽ ♒
Moon in Aquarius

MAY

the first day
of the month
starts with the
ephemeris

☉	11º	♉
☽	12º	♒
☿	17º	♈
♀	2º	♉
♂	0º	♈
♃	24º	♉
♄	17º	♓
♅	22º	♉
♆	29º	♓
♇	2º	♒

MON	TUE	WED
		01
06	07	08
13	14	15
20	21	22
27	28	29

THU	FRI	SAT	SUN
02	03	04	05
09	10	11	12
16	17	18	19
23	24	25	26
30	31		

MAY
01
WED

♀ ♉ □ ♇ ♒
Venus in Taurus squares Pluto in Aquarius

Pluto tells Venus that it's OK to spoil yourself, but don't overspend just to satisfy your needs. We're back to a balanced sense of self-esteem, so it's time to take control of our finances.

Last Quarter 11º Aquarius

New ways of thinking about life will free you from old beliefs. Time to work on the art of letting go, mainly of ideas that belong in the past. Let go of old habits.

MAY
02
THU

♇ St ℞ ♒
Pluto Stations Retrograde 2º Aquarius

As soon as this transit begins, we are ready to take a break, because so much has already been shifted, with many structures having entered a state of decline since January this year. Now it's time to look at our internal structures of power, which are the ones that will be shaken from now until September.

☽ ♓
Moon in Pisces

MAY
03
FRI

♇ ℞ ♒
Pluto Retrograde in Aquarius until 1 September

Take the opportunity to work on whatever you feel addicted to and cannot explain. Also work on your spirituality, as your inner self deserves more of your attention now.

♂ ♈ ⚹ ♇ ℞ ♒
Mars in Aries sextile Pluto Retrograde in Aquarius

Every action has a reaction. This is one of the best times to seek a better understanding of yourself, and any form of therapy or work on self-development will be rewarded. Go for an astral chart consultation!

☽ ♓
Moon in Pisces

MAY
04
SAT

☽ ♈
Moon in Aries

MAY
05
SUN

☽ ♈
Moon in Aries

MAY
06
MON

☽ ♉
Moon in Taurus

פו
י·ה·ו
Meditation for the month of Iyyar
Scan with your eyes from right to left

T A U R U S

8 MAY – 3:22AM (UTC) – NEW MOON 18° TAURUS

Los Angeles (UTC –7) • New York (UTC –4) • London (UTC +1)
Paris (UTC +2) • Sydney (UTC +11)

IN THE NEXT SIX MONTHS I WILL MANIFEST...

Safety Productivity Persistence Values	Stability Financial resources Intimacy Pleasure	Sensuality Self-esteem Body aesthetics Comfort

MAY
07
TUE

☉ ♉ ⚹ ♄ ♓
Sun in Taurus sextile Saturn in Pisces

Maybe your finances are demanding your attention. The unorganized state of these could mean that we do not reach the end of the year having obtained our economic goals. Look into all unnecessary expenditure and commit yourself to not falling into the same trap again.

☽ ♉
Moon in Taurus

MAY
08
WED

● ♉
New Moon 18º Taurus

The New Moon in Taurus announces a new state of finances. You've been treating yourself much better, taking care of your possessions, and you deserve to be rewarded. The Universe says that whatever you wish to manifest is within your power. Set your new financial goals and don't settle for anything less.

MAY
09
THU

☽ ♊
Moon in Gemini

MAY
10
FRI

☽ ♊
Moon in Gemini

MAY
11
SAT

☽ ♋
Moon in Cancer

MAY
12
SUN

☽ ♋
Moon in Cancer

W	T	F	S	S	M	T	W	T	F	S	S	M	T	W	T	F	S	S	M	T	W	T	F	S	S	M	T	W	T	F
1	2	3	4	5	6	7	8	9	10	**11**	**12**	13	14	15	16	17	**18**	**19**	20	21	22	23	24	**25**	**26**	27	28	29	30	31

MAY
13
MON

☉ ☌ ♅ ♉
Sun meets Uranus in Taurus

There are surprises in store for you this week, which starts out unpredictably. You may find new ways to generate extra income by working online on your mobile phone or computer. See what options exist in your market and welcome a new stream of income.

♀ ♉ ✶ ♄ ♓
Venus in Taurus sextile Saturn in Pisces

Everything comes in good time, so put even more dedication into learning about money and the true value of things, because the two are connected. The more you value yourself, the more others will pay for your services. Be confident!

☽ ♌
Moon in Leo

MAY
14
TUE

☽ ♌
Moon in Leo

MAY
15
WED

☿ ♉
Mercury enters Taurus until 3 June

Mercury in Taurus is the best buddy to join you on a course about finances. Start now to organize your expenses and income; the economy is changing and we need to update ourselves, so it's time to learn even more about your worth!

◐ ♌
First Quarter 25º Leo

This Waxing Moon reminds you that your dreams deserve to be realized and that you will be able to reach your goals if you know what your best weapons are and how to use them. The theme of finances gets stronger, as who doesn't dream of founding their own empire and reigning over their own life?

MAY
16
THU

☽ ♍
Moon in Virgo

MAY
17
FRI

☿ ♉ □ ♇ ℞ ♒
Mercury in Taurus squares Pluto Retrograde in Aquarius

Chances are the dialogue between these planets will make you even more obsessed with something you've just discovered. It's a great day to realize where you are sapping yourself of vital energy, money and self-worth. Dive deep into self-analysis to discover your inner treasures.

☽ ♍
Moon in Virgo

MAY
18
SAT

♀ ☌ ♅ ♉
Venus meets Uranus in Taurus

Beautiful surprises await you this Saturday, when anything can happen! You will probably realize that your efforts to improve yourself are now beginning to take effect. You may receive some wonderful news or recognition from your friends, or your partner may be the cherry on the cake today. You deserve it!

☉ ☌ ♃ ♉
Sun meets Jupiter in Taurus

A very beneficial aspect that makes you see how far you've come since the beginning of the year in terms of your self-esteem. This is what the Taurus season is for: to look at both your soul and your physical bank account. Both must be in balance.

☽ ♎
Moon in Libra

MAY
19
SUN

☉ ♉ ✱ ♆ ♓
Sun in Taurus sextile Neptune in Pisces

A Sunday to rest and enjoy the good side of life. Allow yourself to be cared for by your friends or partner. Enjoy good food, laugh and celebrate your recent achievements. Today, enjoy!

☽ ♎
Moon in Libra

MAY
20
MON

☉ ♊
Sun enters Gemini

We start the week with lots of networking to do. The Sun in Gemini brings with it an end-of-season excitement: we are getting ready for another chapter, and for that we need true friends around us. Take this opportunity to arrange meetings and catch up.

☽ ♏
Moon in Scorpio

MAY
21
TUE

☽ ♏
Moon in Scorpio

MAY
22
WED

☉ ♊ △ ♇ ℞ ♒
Sun in Gemini trine Pluto Retrograde in Aquarius

Talk to those above you. This is a great aspect for anyone who wants to get onto the mailing list of their dreams, or to talk to someone they admire a lot and would like to be closer to. Enjoy an unpretentious Wednesday and lay your cards on the table!

☽ ♏
Moon in Scorpio

GEMINI

20 May / 12:59PM (UTC)

GEMINI

MODE Mutable **ELEMENT** Air **RULING PLANET** Mercury

CRYSTAL Agate **BACH FLOWER REMEDY** Cerato

PRINCIPLE Positive **OPPOSITE SIGN** Sagittarius

GEMINI AND SIGNS IN LOVE

Aries	♥ ♥ ♥ ♥ ♡	Libra	♥ ♥ ♥ ♥ ♥
Taurus	♥ ♥ ♡ ♡ ♡	Scorpio	♥ ♡ ♡ ♡ ♡
Gemini	♥ ♥ ♥ ♥ ♥	Sagittarius	♥ ♥ ♥ ♥ ♥
Cancer	♥ ♡ ♡ ♡ ♡	Capricorn	♥ ♡ ♡ ♡ ♡
Leo	♥ ♥ ♥ ♡ ♡	Aquarius	♥ ♥ ♥ ♥ ♡
Virgo	♥ ♥ ♥ ♡ ♡	Pisces	♥ ♥ ♡ ♡ ♡

MANTRA I think **POWER** Versatility

KEYWORD Communicate **ANATOMY** Lungs, Arms, Shoulders, Nervous system

LIGHT
Social
Curious
Adaptable
Expressive
Literary
Inventive
Intelligent

SHADOW
Changeable
Ungrateful
Stupid
Restless
Intriguing
Lacking concentration

MAY
23
THU

♀ ☌ ♃ ♉
Venus meets Jupiter in Taurus

An excellent day for being admired for your work, and great for presenting yourself to the world.

♀ ♉ ✶ ♆ ♓
Venus in Taurus sextile Neptune in Pisces

You've achieved many things, and it's time to blossom even more. Dream even bigger tonight!

♀ ♊
Venus enters Gemini until 17 June

Venus in Gemini wants to explore friendships, and one of yours could turn into a romantic relationship.

♃ ♉ ✶ ♆ ♓
Jupiter in Taurus sextile Neptune in Pisces

Listen to your intuition and take some time to tune in to what your Soul wants to manifest in the world.

○ ♐
Full Moon 2º Sagittarius

A Full Moon of expanding consciousness – now, what is your next adventure?

MAY
24
FRI

☽ ♐
Moon in Sagittarius

MAY
25
SAT

♀ ♊ △ ♇ ℞ ♒
Venus in Gemini trine Pluto Retrograde in Aquarius

It's a fact that this year is changing all our social structures and expanding our horizons, and this aspect allows you to further refine where the right people are for you at this time, and who you want to be with in the coming years. Think about your friendship group and your work.

♃ ♊
Jupiter enters Gemini until 10 June 2025

And here's Jupiter, ready for another adventure and reaffirming that you have a brilliant mind full of groundbreaking ideas that need to be monetized and spread all over this planet. It's a good time to dive into your studies and become a true expert in your field.

☽ ♑
Moon in Capricorn

MAY
26
SUN

☽ ♑
Moon in Capricorn

MAY
27
MON

☽ ♒
Moon in Aquarius

MAY
28
TUE

☿ ♉ ⚹ ♄ ♓
Mercury in Taurus sextile Saturn in Pisces

After the Full Moon and all the excitement of the last few days, Saturn asks Mercury to take the first lessons of a course called "How much are your dreams worth?" You should already know the answer, so write it down here. To what extent are you willing to accomplish all your biggest dreams of 2024?

☽ ♒
Moon in Aquarius

MAY
29
WED

☽ ♒
Moon in Aquarius

MAY
30
THU

◑ ♓
Last Quarter 9º Pisces

A great Thursday for letting go of feeling like a victim and that you do a lot for others without any reward. Time to change your emotional status, so let go of the heavy burden of trying to save the world and focus on your professional and personal ascent. I believe in you!

MAY
31
FRI

☿ ☌ ♅ ♉
Mercury meets Uranus in Taurus

A Friday to speak the truth! Publicize your work, put on a promotion to attract clients, talk about your thesis, your research, and announce your talents to the world. Today is the best day to use the internet megaphone and spread your message.

☽ ♓
Moon in Pisces

W	T	F	**S**	**S**	M	T	W	T	F	**S**	**S**	M	T	W	T	F	**S**	**S**	M	T	W	T	F	**S**	**S**	M	T	W	T	F
1	2	3	**4**	**5**	6	7	8	9	10	**11**	**12**	13	14	15	16	17	**18**	**19**	20	21	22	23	24	**25**	**26**	27	28	29	30	31

JUNE

the first day
of the month
starts with the
ephemeris

☉ 11º ♊
☽ 5º ♈
☿ 26º ♉
♀ 10º ♊
♂ 24º ♈
♃ 1º ♊
♄ 19º ♓
♅ 24º ♉
♆ 29º ♓
♇℞ 2º ♑

MON	TUE	WED
03	04	05
10	11	12
17	18	19
24	25	26

THU	FRI	SAT	SUN
		01	02
06	07	08	09
13	14	15	16
20	21	22	23
27	28	29	30

JUN
01
SAT

☽ ♈
Moon in Aries

JUN
02
SUN

☽ ♈
Moon in Aries

S	S	M	T	W	T	F	S	S	M	T	W	T	F	S	S	M	T	W	T	F	S	S	M	T	W	T	F	S	S
1	**2**	3	4	5	6	7	**8**	**9**	10	11	12	13	14	**15**	**16**	17	18	19	20	21	**22**	**23**	24	25	26	27	28	**29**	**30**

JUN
03
MON

♃ ♊ ✶ ♇ ℞ ♒
Jupiter in Gemini sextile Pluto Retrograde in Aquarius

A heavenly aspect to make you feel on top of the world. It could be that by broadcasting your message you have helped it to reach the right target or the right people! Celebrate your latest achievement and map out the next steps toward fulfilling your ambitions.

☿ ♉ ✶ ♆ ♓
Mercury in Taurus sextile Neptune in Pisces

In his last conversation in Taurus, Mercury accesses even more of your unconscious and downloads more goals onto the physical plane. Can you see how intuitive you've become lately? Meditate on your plan for this year.

☿ ♊
Mercury enters Gemini until 17 June

Having Mercury back in this house will make your mobile messages fizz and pop. Ask for help in dealing with so many invitations and contacts – you will definitely need it!

☽ ♉
Moon in Taurus

JUN
04
TUE

☿ ♊ △ ♇ ℞ ♒
Mercury in Gemini trine Pluto Retrograde in Aquarius

In much the same conversation that Jupiter had yesterday, Mercury sits down today with Pluto to increase the intensity of whatever it is that you wish to express. Good for all work involving writing, presentation, discussion, ideas or marketing. You can do anything today!

☿ ☌ ♃ ♊
Mercury meets Jupiter in Gemini

The conditions are very favourable these days, and it seems that nothing is an obstacle for you. There is a great ability to express yourself verbally, but a dose of discipline is needed to keep on top of all this excitement. Focus on what really matters.

☉ ☌ ♀ ♊
Sun meets Venus in Gemini

The Sun and Venus in Gemini make for a great party and excellent social situations. Take advantage of the moment to meet even more people.

☽ ♉
Moon in Taurus

JUN
05
WED

☽ ♊
Moon in Gemini

JUN
06
THU

● ♊
New Moon 16º Gemini

The most intense week of the year is coming to an end, but the New Moon indicates that many people are entering your life. Say goodbye to shallow relationships and focus even more on the friendships that you value and which take you to the next level. Have fun!

רז
י·ו·ה·ה
Meditation for the month of Sivan
Scan with your eyes from right to left

G E M I N I

6 JUNE – 12:38PM (UTC) – NEW MOON 16° GEMINI

Los Angeles (UTC –7) • New York (UTC –4) • London (UTC +1)
Paris (UTC +2) • Sydney (UTC +11)

IN THE NEXT SIX MONTHS I WILL MANIFEST...

Flexibility Adaptability Cunning Persuasion	Social work Curiosity Communication Quickness	Connecting people Learning Self-expression Youth

JUN
07
FRI

☽ ♋
Moon in Cancer

JUN
08
SAT

♀ ♊ □ ♄ ♓
Venus in Gemini squares Saturn in Pisces

The hustle and bustle was so much that Saturn had to come and establish some order. Now he is talking about emotional responsibility, and while you are opening up to more people each day, you need to make clear what your intentions are with each of them. Don't fall into an ego trip!

☽ ♋
Moon in Cancer

JUN
09
SUN

♂ ♉
Mars enters Taurus until 20 July

The days have flown by this week and lots of new information should be coming your way now! Mars entering Taurus makes you process all the information so that it becomes something concrete in the future. Take action now.

☉ ♊ □ ♄ ♓
Sun in Gemini squares Saturn in Pisces

It may be Sunday, but with these two aspects in the sky, I advise you to schedule your next week and place some limits on the party. We're approaching the Solstice, where energy levels will be high, so save some energy for when the party really starts.

☽ ♌
Moon in Leo

JUN
10
MON

☽ ♌
Moon in Leo

JUN
11
TUE

♂ ♉ □ ♇ ℞ ♒
Mars in Taurus squares Pluto Retrograde in Aquarius

Mars in Taurus wants to cut down on the excesses of the last month, but his conversation with Pluto could turn you into a slightly aggressive and intolerant person. Take into consideration the feelings of the people around you.

☽ ♌
Moon in Leo

JUN
12
WED

☿ ♊ □ ♄ ♓
Mercury in Gemini squares Saturn in Pisces

Another aspect that puts limits on your interaction with others. You may have a very agitated social life and need some time alone. Enjoy this time and know that everything will be available to you whenever you want it.

☽ ♍
Moon in Virgo

JUN
13
THU

☽ ♍
Moon in Virgo

JUN
14
FRI

☉ ☌ ☿ ♊
Sun meets Mercury in Gemini

Another wonderful Friday to promote your products and services or host a big party! Even better if you can congratulate those who have been with you since the beginning of this process. Celebrate with your team!

◐ ♍
First Quarter 23º Virgo

The Waxing Moon brings you back to your routines, which put in place the structure you need to grow even stronger. When the party is over, go back to the worksheets, to the detailed calculations, and establish a time to start and finish your work. Attend to your personal needs this coming weekend.

JUN
15
SAT

☽ ♎
Moon in Libra

JUN
16
SUN

☽ ♎
Moon in Libra

JUN
17
MON

♀ ♊ □ ♆ ♓
Venus in Gemini squares Neptune in Pisces

Another busy Monday in the sky! Who is ready for a shocking dose of reality?

☿ ♊ □ ♆ ♓
Mercury in Gemini squares Neptune in Pisces

Venus and Mercury are in serious conversation with Neptune, which makes you take off those rose-tinted glasses and see new truths. Beware of gossip and check the facts before speaking out.

♀ ♋
Venus enters Cancer until 11 July

After getting any illusions out of the way, Venus and Mercury enter Cancer together to heighten our sensitivity even more. We now search for soul connections.

☿ ♋
Mercury enters Cancer until 2 July

☽ ♏
Moon in Scorpio

JUN
18
TUE

☽ ♏
Moon in Scorpio

JUN
19
WED

☽ ♐
Moon in Sagittarius

JUN
20
THU

☉ ♊ □ ♆ ♓
Sun in Gemini squares Neptune in Pisces

Another wake-up call concerning the fantasies you've created in your mind. Perhaps you are not seeing reality as it is, so add a measure of balance to your intentions and try to come back down to Earth this Solstice!

☉ ♋
Sun enters Cancer

We may become needy and want to feel a sense of belonging in life. The Sun in Cancer invites you to plunge into self-care, to nourish your soul and nurture your friends with affection. Who is important to you at this time? Prepare a pie or make jam with seasonal fruit and gift it to friends this season.

Summer Solstice – Litha North Hemisphere
Winter Solstice – Yule South Hemisphere

☽ ♐
Moon in Sagittarius

JUN
21
FRI

☿ ♋ ✶ ♂ ♉
Mercury in Cancer sextile Mars in Taurus

A good day for research and for evaluating your trajectory so far. You are building your dream future, so celebrate each achievement without losing focus. Connect with the process: the best thing about reaching your destination is the experiences along the way.

☽ ♑
Moon in Capricorn

JUN
22
SAT

○ ♑
Full Moon 1º Capricorn

A Full Moon for expressing emotional security. It wasn't easy, but today you already feel much more confident in dreaming big because you know your worth. Celebrate your victories with those who give you the greatest support in your challenges.

CANCER

20 June / 8:51PM (UTC)

CANCER

MODE Cardinal **ELEMENT** Water **RULING PLANET** Moon

CRYSTAL Moonstone **BACH FLOWER REMEDY** Clematis

PRINCIPLE Negative **OPPOSITE SIGN** Capricorn

CANCER AND SIGNS IN LOVE

Aries	♥ ♡ ♡ ♡ ♡	Libra	♥ ♥ ♥ ♡ ♡
Taurus	♥ ♥ ♥ ♥ ♡	Scorpio	♥ ♥ ♥ ♥ ♥
Gemini	♥ ♡ ♡ ♡ ♡	Sagittarius	♥ ♡ ♡ ♡ ♡
Cancer	♥ ♥ ♥ ♥ ♡	Capricorn	♥ ♥ ♥ ♥ ♡
Leo	♥ ♥ ♥ ♡ ♡	Aquarius	♥ ♥ ♡ ♡ ♡
Virgo	♥ ♥ ♥ ♥ ♡	Pisces	♥ ♥ ♥ ♥ ♥

MANTRA I feel **POWER** Devotion

KEYWORD Feeling **ANATOMY** Stomach, Pancreas, Chest

LIGHT

Tenacious
Maternal
Sensitive
Retentive
Helpful to others
Friendly
Emotional
Patriotic
Traditional
Good memory

SHADOW

Touchy
Hurts easily
Negative
Manipulative
Too cautious
Lazy
Selfish
Self-pitying
Insecure
Passive

JUN
23
SUN

☽ ♑
Moon in Capricorn

JUN
24
MON

☽ ♒
Moon in Aquarius

S	S	M	T	W	T	F	S	S	M	T	W	T	F	S	S	M	T	W	T	F	S	S	M	T	W	T	F	S	S
1	**2**	3	4	5	6	7	**8**	**9**	10	11	12	13	14	**15**	**16**	17	18	19	20	21	**22**	**23**	24	25	26	27	28	**29**	**30**

JUN
25
TUE

☽ ♒
Moon in Aquarius

JUN
26
WED

☿ ♋ △ ♄ ♓
Mercury in Cancer trine Saturn in Pisces

To achieve our goals and fulfil our personal mission this year, it is essential to be able to count on our soul family. Who are the people who are holding your hand in the best and worst moments? Celebrate with them.

☽ ♓
Moon in Pisces

JUN
27
THU

☽ ♓
Moon in Pisces

JUN
28
FRI

◑ ♈
Last Quarter 7º Aries

Let go of that selfish attitude of yours; it's time to open up to the world and harmonize together. Time to release anything that is holding you back from connecting with those you love. Show your love today!

S	S	M	T	W	T	F	S	S	M	T	W	T	F	S	S	M	T	W	T	F	S	S	M	T	W	T	F	S	S
1	2	3	4	5	6	7	8	9	10	11	12	13	14	15	16	17	18	19	20	21	22	23	24	25	26	27	28	29	30

JUN
29
SAT

♀ ♋ ✶ ♂ ♉
Venus in Cancer sextile Mars in Taurus

A Saturday of loving and being loved! Venus is melting and Mars is your safe harbour at this time. If you are single, invite people into your private space. Our greatest teaching here is to learn to feel and vibrate with love. Go deep!

♄ St ℞ ♓
Saturn Stations Retrograde 19º Pisces

At the same time as Venus is building castles in the air, Saturn asks you not to commit so deeply in the next months. Wait for the dust of passion to settle; in the meantime, observe your emotions.

☽ ♈
Moon in Aries

JUN
30
SUN

☿ ♋ ✶ ♅ ♉
Mercury in Cancer sextile Uranus in Taurus

Your intuition is running wild and you want to share with others what you're feeling. Do this just to make sure you were right.

♄ ℞ ♓
Saturn Retrograde in Pisces until 15 November

Between now and November, revisit all agreements and everything that has been agreed or needs your signature, as all major decisions in your life are going through a review. Dive deep into what your heart is telling you.

☽ ♉
Moon in Taurus

S	S	M	T	W	T	F	S	S	M	T	W	T	F	S	S	M	T	W	T	F	S	S	M	T	W	T	F	S	S
1	**2**	3	4	5	6	7	**8**	**9**	10	11	12	13	14	**15**	**16**	17	18	19	20	21	**22**	**23**	24	25	26	27	28	**29**	**30**

JULY

the first day of the month starts with the ephemeris

☉	10º	♋
☽	14º	♉
☿	27º	♋
♀	17º	♋
♂	16º	♉
♃	8º	♊
♄ ℞	19º	♓
♅	25º	♉
♆	29º	♓
♇ ℞	1º	♒

MON	TUE	WED
01	02	03
08	09	10
15	16	17
22	23	24
29	30	31

THU	FRI	SAT	SUN
04	05	06	07
11	12	13	14
18	19	20	21
25	26	27	28

JUL
01
MON

☽ ♉
Moon in Taurus

JUL
02
TUE

☿ ♌
Mercury enters Leo until 25 July

The season of emotional drama has begun. Our attention is only on those who want us around. We may be a little too enchanted with so much attention, and it's nice to feel that way. Just guard against the tendency to overreact and don't get too worked up about anyone.

♆ St ℞ ♓
Neptune Stations Retrograde 29º Pisces

Today is when Neptune is preparing for his annual hibernation. It is a moment to feel our feet coming down to Earth in areas that were previously very far from reality. What a relief!

☿ ♋ △ ♆ ℞ ♓
Mercury in Cancer trine Neptune Retrograde in Pisces

Your sixth sense is very sharp, with charm and dazzle. You are feeling everything so clearly that you can read people very well, and at the same time they feel bewitched by you. Enjoy the magick!

☽ ♊
Moon in Gemini

JUL
03
WED

♆ ℞ ♓
Neptune Retrograde in Pisces until 7 December

A great time to move forward with creative projects. Deepen your connection with your Inner Master, pray in your own temple and honour yourself.

♀ ♋ △ ♄ ℞ ♓
Venus in Cancer trine Saturn Retrograde in Pisces

Evaluate your emotions; decide if there is a need to let go of an illusion, or solidify a relationship. Do not attach yourself to things that are already past.

☿ ♌ ☍ ♇ ℞ ♒
Mercury in Leo opposite Pluto Retrograde in Aquarius

With a restless mind and intense thoughts, try not to push yourself too hard in power games, and do not take pressure from others too seriously. Open your mind and try to filter out the negative things you may hear about yourself.

☽ ♊
Moon in Gemini

JUL
04
THU

☽ ♋
Moon in Cancer

M	T	W	T	F	**S**	**S**	M	T	W	T	F	**S**	**S**	M	T	W	T	F	**S**	**S**	M	T	W	T	F	**S**	**S**	M	T	W
1	2	3	4	5	**6**	**7**	8	9	10	11	12	**13**	**14**	15	16	17	18	19	**20**	**21**	22	23	24	25	26	**27**	**28**	29	30	31

JUL
05
FRI

♂ ♉ ✶ ♄ ℞ ♓
Mars in Taurus sextile Saturn Retrograde in Pisces

Now you can calmly evaluate why you worked so hard for a situation. Review your level of commitment, and remember that building is about constancy. Are you really willing to let go of everything you've already achieved internally?

● ♋
New Moon 14º Cancer

New Moon of the nest, of the bubble of love, of your home. Where do you feel most welcome and comfortable? Do you feel calm and serene with your family members? What can you change to live in such an environment? How would you like your bonds to develop?

JUL
06
SAT

☽ ♋
Moon in Cancer

זזת
ה·ו·ה·י
Meditation for the month of Tamuz
Scan with your eyes from right to left

CANCER

5 JULY – 10:57PM (UTC) – NEW MOON 14° CANCER

Los Angeles (UTC −7) • New York (UTC −4) • London (UTC +1)
Paris (UTC +2) • Sydney (UTC +11)

IN THE NEXT SIX MONTHS I WILL MANIFEST...

Nourish Nutrition Sentimental Emotional patterns	Past memories Protection Self-preservation Care for the home	Cooking Ancestral heritage Romance Intuition

JUL
07
SUN

☽ ♌
Moon in Leo

JUL
08
MON

♀ ♋ ✱ ♅ ♉
Venus in Cancer sextile Uranus in Taurus

You oscillate between moments of complete happiness and commitment and moments of dissociation and isolation from certain people or situations. Look at this and observe how you feel with each group of people. Breakthroughs in love are quite possible.

☿ ♌ ✱ ♃ ♊
Mercury in Leo sextile Jupiter in Gemini

You want to reign and you already have exactly the group of people that you deserve. Your friends, your followers, your tribe give you the support you so badly need, so treat them with care, know how to lead in the storm and don't try too hard, as you naturally shine.

☽ ♌
Moon in Leo

M	T	W	T	F	S	S	M	T	W	T	F	S	S	M	T	W	T	F	S	S	M	T	W	T	F	S	S	M	T	W
1	2	3	4	5	**6**	**7**	8	9	10	11	12	**13**	**14**	15	16	17	18	19	**20**	**21**	22	23	24	25	26	**27**	**28**	29	30	31

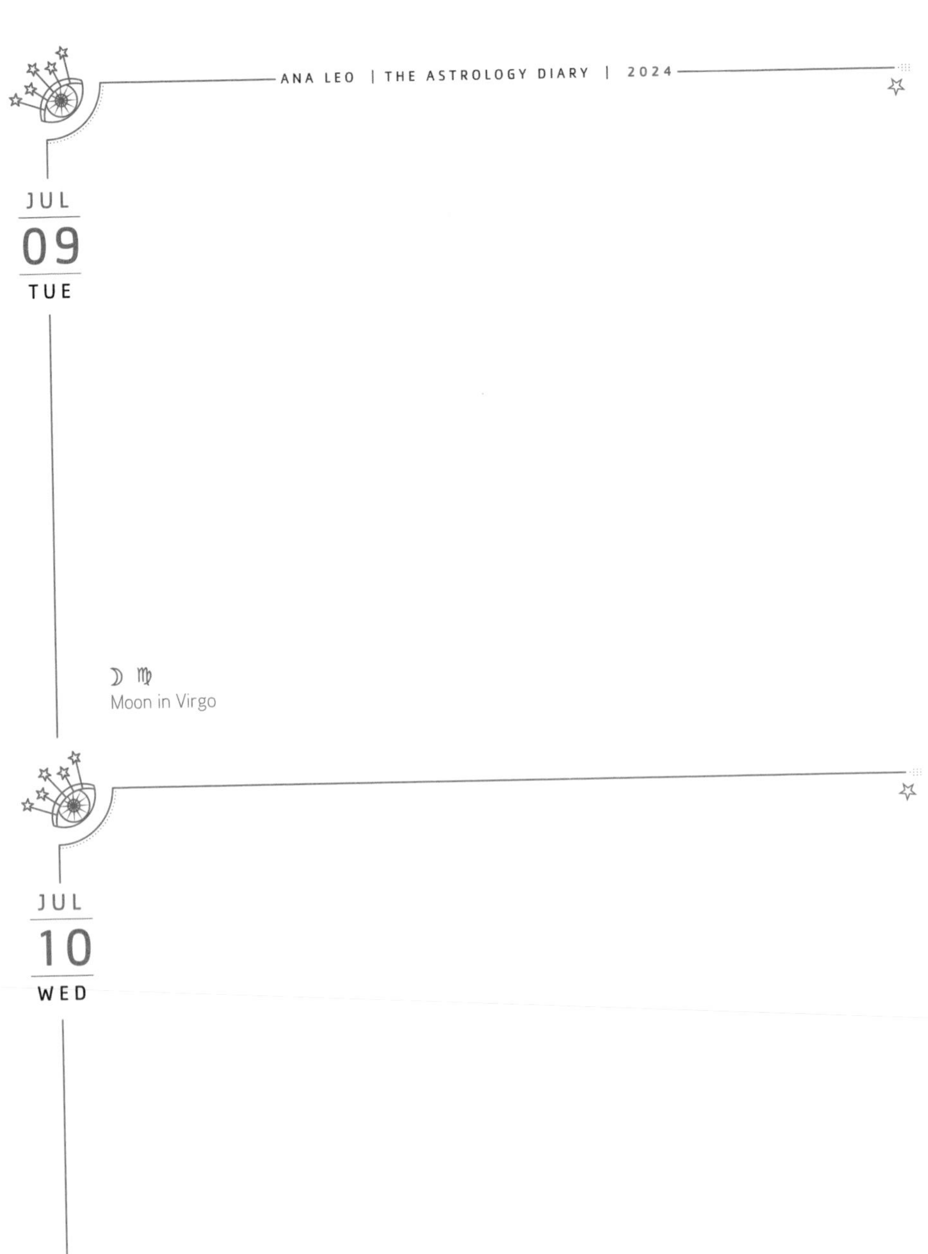

JUL
09
TUE

☽ ♍
Moon in Virgo

JUL
10
WED

☽ ♍
Moon in Virgo

M	T	W	T	F	S	S	M	T	W	T	F	S	S	M	T	W	T	F	S	S	M	T	W	T	F	S	S	M	T	W
1	2	3	4	5	6	7	8	9	10	11	12	13	14	15	16	17	18	19	20	21	22	23	24	25	26	27	28	29	30	31

JUL
11
THU

☉ ♋ △ ♄ ℞ ♓
Sun in Cancer trine Saturn Retrograde in Pisces

Something you've been wanting to feel for a long time starts knocking on your door. A warm feeling, a caress from someone close, a validation. Let the nourishment in!

♀ ♋ △ ♆ ℞ ♓
Venus in Cancer trine Neptune Retrograde in Pisces

Ready to experience that emotion, your heart feels full of hope again. Today is a memorable day, ideal for living, reading or watching a romance. Keep an eye on your spending and experience a great love affair – even with yourself!

♀ ♌
Venus enters Leo until 5 August

The desire will be to conquer everything and everyone in the room, as this Venus in Leo wants nothing less than lots of gold and glitter.

☽ ♍
Moon in Virgo

JUL
12
FRI

♀ ♌ ☍ ♇ ℞ ♒
Venus in Leo opposite Pluto Retrograde in Aquarius

A tussle between freedom and commitment, you want everyone at your feet, but you won't admit to surrendering to another, and this creates imbalance. Sometimes we need to look at the whole picture and not just our personal desires. Beware of attracting attention in a way that is not positive for you.

☽ ♎
Moon in Libra

JUL
13
SAT

◐ ♎
First Quarter 22º Libra

A good Saturday to make the house even more appealing, or to receive visitors. Time to work on how you want to feel inside your home and with your loved ones. Create something beautiful.

JUL
14
SUN

☽ ♏
Moon in Scorpio

JUL
15
MON

♂ ☌ ♅ ♉
Mars meets Uranus in Taurus

We start the week by paying more attention to our bodies. We may be a little clumsy and accidents might happen easily. Take care of your surroundings and be patient with others. Everything comes at the right time!

☽ ♏
Moon in Scorpio

JUL
16
TUE

☽ ♏
Moon in Scorpio

JUL
17
WED

☽ ♐
Moon in Sagittarius

JUL
18
THU

☉ ♋ ✶ ♅ ♉
Sun in Cancer sextile Uranus in Taurus

Excellent time to come out of your shell, revealing your real worth, and to value your own talents, research and memory. Realize all the personal expansion you are creating for yourself, and vibrate loudly with the Universe to tune in to the best opportunities.

☽ ♐
Moon in Sagittarius

JUL
19
FRI

☽ ♑
Moon in Capricorn

JUL
20
SAT

♂ ♉ ⚹ ♆ ℞ ♓
Mars in Taurus sextile Neptune Retrograde in Pisces

A good Saturday for receiving compliments and telling others about your achievements. Feel the charm exude from within and realize how much more you can achieve. Take small risks and experiment with your own energy.

♂ ♊
Mars enters Gemini until 4 September

We have 45 days now in which to follow up the instincts of our curiosity and see how far we can go. An impulse for adventure and challenge catches your attention. Develop your focus on one of your goals and enjoy a sense of complete fulfilment at the end of this season.

☽ ♑
Moon in Capricorn

JUL
21
SUN

♀ ♌ ⚹ ♃ ♊
Venus in Leo sextile Jupiter in Gemini

This socializing Sunday, Venus in Leo wants to shine and have fun. Luck seems to be on your side, so come out to play! An adventure park, a beach, a picnic – open yourself up to it all.

☿ ♌ □ ♅ ♉
Mercury in Leo squares Uranus in Taurus

Don't reject opportunities to enjoy life through thinking you are superior, or by not appreciating the real value of each situation. Try not to look down on things from the top of your castle!

○ ♑
Full Moon 29º Capricorn

At the second Full Moon in Capricorn of the year, it's easier now to understand that your confidence blossoms from the pride and love you feel for your whole story. At this beautiful end-of-month celebration, feel on top of the world – you've climbed that mountain!

JUL
22
MON

☉ ♋ △ ♆ ℞ ♓
Sun in Cancer trine Neptune Retrograde in Pisces

After a weekend of so many emotions, it will be hard to get out of the bubble and get back to real life. Make the most of your free time to call your friends and catch up on old times.

♂ ♊ △ ♇ ℞ ♒
Mars in Gemini trine Pluto Retrograde in Aquarius

Your powers of persuasion are at their peak. Take advantage of the moment to convince as many people as possible that your idea is achievable, as you can count on your friends to spread your word.

☉ ♌
Sun enters Leo

To brighten things up even more, the Sun rises in the kingdom of Leo, and we gain a greater exuberance, as if the colours were more vivid. Make the most of this wave of optimism and speak from the heart.

☽ ♒
Moon in Aquarius

LEO

22 July / 7:44AM (UTC)

LEO

MODE Fixed **ELEMENT** Fire **RULING PLANET** Sun

CRYSTAL Ruby **BACH FLOWER REMEDY** Vervain

PRINCIPLE Positive **OPPOSITE SIGN** Aquarius

LEO AND SIGNS IN LOVE

Aries	♥ ♥ ♥ ♥ ♡	Libra	♥ ♥ ♥ ♥ ♡
Taurus	♥ ♥ ♥ ♡ ♡	Scorpio	♥ ♡ ♡ ♡ ♡
Gemini	♥ ♥ ♥ ♥ ♡	Sagittarius	♥ ♥ ♥ ♥ ♥
Cancer	♥ ♥ ♡ ♡ ♡	Capricorn	♥ ♥ ♡ ♡ ♡
Leo	♥ ♥ ♥ ♡ ♡	Aquarius	♥ ♥ ♥ ♥ ♥
Virgo	♥ ♥ ♡ ♡ ♡	Pisces	♥ ♡ ♡ ♡ ♡

MANTRA I want **POWER** Magnetism

KEYWORD Creation **ANATOMY** Heart, Back, Spine

LIGHT
Vain
Idealistic
Ambitious
Creative
Majestic
Generous
Romantic
Optimistic
Self-Ccnfident

SHADOW
Dramatic
Worried about status
Proud
Arrogant
Afraid of ridicule
Cruel
Pretentious
Autocratic
Centre of attention

JUL
23
TUE

☉ ♌ ☍ ♇ ℞ ♒
Sun in Leo opposite Pluto Retrograde in Aquarius

With his power and intensity, Pluto wants to deflate the ego of this Leo and say that the lion's kingdom must include everyone. Listen to your heart and let go of any sort of manipulation. An excellent moment for a more humble look at your life.

☽ ♓
Moon in Pisces

JUL
24
WED

☽ ♓
Moon in Pisces

JUL
25
THU

☿ ♍
Mercury enters Virgo until 15 August (will retrograde)

Leo season wants to bring out all that brilliance, in every respect. Mercury in one of his houses will pay attention to any details that keep you from having a fair and honest conversation. Return to your routines.

☽ ♈
Moon in Aries

JUL
26
FRI

☉ ♌ ✶ ♂ ♊
Sun in Leo sextile Mars in Gemini

There are so many talents you would like to share, and it seems there is not enough time for many of the activities you would like to do. Focus on what makes you shine without dazzling others – the shine that is only yours.

☽ ♈
Moon in Aries

JUL
27
SAT

☽ ♉
Moon in Taurus

JUL
28
SUN

◑ ♉
Last Quarter 5º Taurus

What are the feelings, people or situations that prevent all your talents from shining? A wonderful time to be very sure of everything you need to do in order to finally let go.

M	T	W	T	F	**S**	**S**	M	T	W	T	F	**S**	**S**	M	T	W	T	F	**S**	**S**	M	T	W	T	F	**S**	**S**	M	T	W
1	2	3	4	5	**6**	**7**	8	9	10	11	12	**13**	**14**	15	16	17	18	19	**20**	**21**	22	23	24	25	26	**27**	**28**	29	30	31

JUL
29
MON

☽ ♊
Moon in Gemini

JUL
30
TUE

☽ ♊
Moon in Gemini

M	T	W	T	F	S	S	M	T	W	T	F	S	S	M	T	W	T	F	S	S	M	T	W	T	F	S	S	M	T	W
1	2	3	4	5	6	7	8	9	10	11	12	13	14	15	16	17	18	19	20	21	22	23	24	25	26	27	28	29	30	31

[illegible]

31

WED

☽ ♊

Moon in Gemini

M	T	W	T	F	S	S	M	T	W	T	F	S	S	M	T	W	T	F	S	S	M	T	W	T	F	S	S	M	T	W
1	2	3	4	5	6	7	8	9	10	11	12	13	14	15	16	17	18	19	20	21	22	23	24	25	26	27	28	29	30	31

AUGUST

the first day of the month starts with the ephemeris

☉	9º	♌
☽	5º	♋
☿	3º	♍
♀	25º	♌
♂	8º	♊
♃	14º	♊
♄℞	19º	♓
♅	27º	♉
♆℞	29º	♓
♇℞	1º	♒

MON	TUE	WED
05	06	07
12	13	14
19	20	21
26	27	28

THU	FRI	SAT	SUN
01	02	03	04
08	09	10	11
15	16	17	18
22	23	24	25
29	30	31	

AUG
01
THU

☽ ♋
Moon in Cancer

AUG
02
FRI

♀ ♌ □ ♅ ♉
Venus in Leo squares Uranus in Taurus

A Friday of stormy passions – suddenly something or someone catches your eye and you don't recognize yourself among so much dazzle. The heady brew of seduction overflows, and you want to get out of one relationship and jump straight into another. Hold your nerve and wait until you are more at peace and able to make up your mind.

☽ ♋
Moon in Cancer

כט
ה·י·ו·ה
Meditation for the month of Av
Scan with your eyes from right to left

L E O

4 AUGUST - 11:13AM (UTC) - NEW MOON 12° LEO

Los Angeles (UTC −7) • New York (UTC −4) • London (UTC +1)
Paris (UTC +2) • Sydney (UTC +11)

IN THE NEXT SIX MONTHS I WILL MANIFEST...

Being Queen or King Shining with the heart Talents Creative projects	Pride Generosity Self-confidence Vanity	Hair care Power Self-expression Individuality

AUG
03
SAT

☽ ♌
Moon in Leo

AUG
04
SUN

● ♌
New Moon 12º Leo

A New Moon of creativity and the inner child. Seeing as we are all creative in one area of our lives or another, consider where you want to explore your own creative urges more. Where is your stage? In what area of your life do you definitely shine? Focus on the future.

AUG
05
MON

♀ ♍
Venus enters Virgo until 29 August

When Venus is transiting Mercury's house in the same season as he is reviewing everything, this is a great sign that we're not messing around. Our professional interests come to the surface, and we adjust our routines to deliver everything with excellence. Also a great time to consult a nutritionist.

☿ St ℞ ♍
Mercury Stations Retrograde in 4º Virgo

The week begins with a bit of work as Mercury decides to look at the smallest details and fix what is not working perfectly anymore. Take this opportunity to classify and catalogue all your best ideas.

☽ ♍
Moon in Virgo

AUG
06
TUE

☿ ℞ ♍
Mercury Retrograde in Virgo until 15 August

We will have ten days in which to examine our way of facing the world. When he returns to Leo, perhaps this Mercury will rethink some of last month's attitudes that were a little over the top. We will bring some humility into the process and move on!

☽ ♍
Moon in Virgo

AUG
07
WED

☉ ♌ ✳ ♃ ♊
Sun in Leo sextile Jupiter in Gemini

Now that it seems everything is working in your favour, your popularity is growing, your thoughts are more positive and fortune is on your side, enjoy this moment – but also keep matters in perspective, because you may tend to overdo it and do excessive things because you are so happy. Save some enthusiasm for the end of the month.

☽ ♍
Moon in Virgo

AUG
08
THU

☿ ℞ ☌ ♀ ♍
Mercury Retrograde meets Venus in Virgo

During this meeting of planetary powers that seek out the best, we are pickier than ever, looking at everything through a magnifying glass. Good for all that detailed work, but watch your self-criticism and exaggerated judgement; we are in a phase of much expansion, and maybe you are attached to things that are so small that they are not worth the stress. Analyse your desires!

☽ ♎
Moon in Libra

AUG
09
FRI

☽ ♎
Moon in Libra

AUG
10
SAT

☽ ♏
Moon in Scorpio

T	F	S	S	M	T	W	T	F	S	S	M	T	W	T	F	S	S	M	T	W	T	F	S	S	M	T	W	T	F	S
1	2	**3**	**4**	5	6	7	8	9	**10**	**11**	12	13	14	15	16	**17**	**18**	19	20	21	22	23	**24**	**25**	26	27	28	29	30	**31**

AUG
11
SUN

☽ ♏
Moon in Scorpio

AUG
12
MON

◐ ♏
First Quarter 20º Scorpio

To achieve Leo's intentions, we have to dive a little deeper into our fears and insecurities. Is there any old conditioning that needs to be eliminated now? Heal yourself by expressing yourself authentically.

AUG
13
TUE

☽ ♐
Moon in Sagittarius

AUG
14
WED

♂ ☌ ♃ ♊
Mars meets Jupiter in Gemini

There are so many things to be done and so many elaborate ideas, that it's very easy to get lost in the excitement if you become caught up in hours of discussion or brainstorming. With Mercury retrograde, it's a good idea to review all attitudes and think twice before you act, as the pace moves so fast that you're more likely to fall down. Take a long, deep breath.

☽ ♐
Moon in Sagittarius

AUG
15
THU

☿ ℞ ♌
Mercury Retrograde goes back to Leo until 9 September

This is the chance you needed to redeem yourself for your inflated ego of the last month. Maybe you've overstepped the mark with some people and it's time to apologize and put your pride aside.

☽ ♑
Moon in Capricorn

AUG
16
FRI

♂ ♊ □ ♄ ℞ ♓
Mars in Gemini squares Saturn Retrograde in Pisces

Frustration and delay in realizing dreams. A Friday to work on patience, persistence and focus. Perhaps you are trying to reach an imaginary target that is not quite achievable. Review your strategy and avoid the easy path. Persist in pursuing the dream but not at the cost of of accomplishing your goal.

☽ ♑
Moon in Capricorn

AUG
17
SAT

☽ ♒
Moon in Aquarius

AUG
18
SUN

☿ ℞ ♌ □ ♅ ♉
Mercury Retrograde in Leo squares Uranus in Taurus

Something you disregarded a month ago makes sense again, and now that you are a little more humble, maybe it's the right time to work on what you already know so well. Your intuition is strong, so trust your thoughts, but only give your final answer when Mercury turns direct.

☉ ☌ ☿ ℞ ♌
Sun meets Mercury Retrograde in Leo

We've reached the midpoint of the retrograde, and now it's easier to plan your next steps. Get ready for the week starting tomorrow.

♀ ♍ □ ♃ ♊
Venus in Virgo squares Jupiter in Gemini

Financial control will be fundamental in order to reach your greatest creative potential. Establish limits in life and in love.

☽ ♒
Moon in Aquarius

AUG
19
MON

♀ ♍ ☍ ♄ ℞ ♓
Venus in Virgo opposite Saturn Retrograde in Pisces

If you are already in a relationship, this aspect could strengthen your union even more. Or you may distance y ourself and focus on your work.

☉ ♌ □ ♅ ♉
Sun in Leo squares Uranus in Taurus

You want lasting change in your life, and this is the time to go for it, rather than just wait.

♃ ♊ □ ♄ ℞ ♓
Jupiter in Gemini squares Saturn Retrograde in Pisces

It's too easy to take on too much responsibility and feel completely exhausted as a result. Learn to say no and establish boundaries in your friendships and work groups.

○ ♒
Full Moon 27º Aquarius

Full Moon of the Twin Souls, this year is different! To find the right partnership, you must learn to negotiate the relationship better and not accept everything from everyone. It's not the best day for romance, but your attitude today can change all the connections in your life.

AUG
20
TUE

☽ ♓
Moon in Pisces

AUG
21
WED

☽ ♈
Moon in Aries

AUG
22
THU

☉ ♍
Sun enters Virgo

The Sun entering an Earth sign makes us want to be in the middle of nature, while enjoying the nuances of our personalities. This is one of the best moments to serve humanity in a responsible way. Take care of your body, and start a physical and energetic detox this month.

☽ ♈
Moon in Aries

VIRGO

22 August / 2:55PM (UTC)

VIRGO

MODE Mutable **ELEMENT** Earth **RULING PLANET** Mercury

CRYSTAL Peridot **BACH FLOWER REMEDY** Centaury

PRINCIPLE Negative **OPPOSITE SIGN** Pisces

VIRGO AND SIGNS IN LOVE

Aries	♥ ♥ ♥ ♡ ♡	Libra	♥ ♥ ♥ ♡ ♡
Taurus	♥ ♥ ♥ ♥ ♥	Scorpio	♥ ♥ ♥ ♥ ♡
Gemini	♥ ♥ ♡ ♡ ♡	Sagittarius	♥ ♡ ♡ ♡ ♡
Cancer	♥ ♥ ♥ ♥ ♡	Capricorn	♥ ♥ ♥ ♥ ♡
Leo	♥ ♥ ♡ ♡ ♡	Aquarius	♥ ♡ ♡ ♡ ♡
Virgo	♥ ♥ ♥ ♡ ♡	Pisces	♥ ♥ ♥ ♥ ♥

MANTRA I analyze **POWER** Practicality

KEYWORD Dedication **ANATOMY** Intestines, Liver, Vesicle, Lower plexus

LIGHT
Diligent
Scientific
Methodical
Discriminative
Fact-finding
Demanding
Clean
Pursues perfection

SHADOW
Critical
Stingy
Melancholic
Egocentric
Afraid of disease and poverty
Difficult to please
Pedantic
Sceptical

AUG
23
FRI

♀ ♍ □ ♂ ♊
Venus in Virgo squares Mars in Gemini

The cosmic couple find themselves in the houses of Mercury while it is retrograde. It can be confusing to try to express our feelings and reach any conclusions in matters of the heart. Passions may be running high, but the moment calls for more certainty. Wait a few more days!

☽ ♈
Moon in Aries

AUG
24
SAT

☿ ℞ ♌ ✶ ♂ ♊
Mercury Retrograde in Leo sextile Mars in Gemini

Patience and effort seem to be far from you at this time. Take a few steps back to remember how you were feeling in July and don't lose focus on what you want to manifest this year!

☽ ♉
Moon in Taurus

AUG
25
SUN

☽ ♉
Moon in Taurus

AUG
26
MON

◑ ♊
Last Quarter 3º Gemini

This Waning Moon makes you even more curious to know what you are missing out on with respect to the choices you make. Everything that is meant to be yours will remain so – don't worry!

AUG
27
TUE

♀ ♍ △ ♅ ♉
Venus in Virgo trine Uranus in Taurus

Your recent self-care can bring you even more rewards and self-esteem. Unexpected gains can appear like magick. Stay focused on the project of not giving up on yourself and your needs; answer the call of your body and spirit now.

☽ ♊
Moon in Gemini

AUG
28
WED

♀ ♍ ☍ ♆ ℞ ♓
Venus in Virgo opposite Neptune Retrograde in Pisces

Today you can – even without meaning to – fall into the trap of self-sabotage. Possibilities include wanting to skip the rules you set down for yourself, or trying to cheat your way through. Otherwise a relaxed day, great for enjoying yourself with your partner!

☿ St D ♌
Mercury Stations Direct in 21º Leo

Wait one more day to define your priorities until the end of the year. Listen once again to your heart and be generous with the people around you.

☽ ♋
Moon in Cancer

AUG
29
THU

♀ ♎
Venus enters Libra until 23 September

Venus in Libra wants to spread beauty in all relationships. Best time to get friends together and attend social events, as with Mercury direct it's easier to respond with impartiality and not get into trouble. All the best!

♀ ♎ △ ♇ ℞ ♒
Venus in Libra trine Pluto Retrograde in Aquarius

Venus receives divine help from Pluto, wanting to bring you favourable social circumstances in a short time. Your appearance can attract a lot of attention, so take care of yourself this month.

☿ D ♌
Mercury Direct in Leo

After a long stretch of 24 days that left us stunned, now we can wake up our minds with our hearts. From today you can handle all the paperwork that has awaited your decisions. Life must go on!

☽ ♋
Moon in Cancer

AUG
30
FRI

☽ ♌
Moon in Leo

AUG
31
SAT

☽ ♌
Moon in Leo

T	F	S	S	M	T	W	T	F	S	S	M	T	W	T	F	S	S	M	T	W	T	F	S	S	M	T	W	T	F	S
1	2	3	4	5	6	7	8	9	10	11	12	13	14	15	16	17	18	19	20	21	22	23	24	25	26	27	28	29	30	31

SEPTEMBER

the first day of the month starts with the ephemeris

☉	9º	♍
☽	22º	♌
☿	22º	♌
♀	3º	♎
♂	28º	♊
♃	19º	♊
♄℞	16º	♓
♅	27º	♉
♆℞	29º	♓
♇℞	0º	♒

MON	TUE	WED
02	03	04
09	10	11
16	17	18
23	24	25
30		

THU	FRI	SAT	SUN
			01
05	06	07	08
12	13	14	15
19	20	21	22
26	27	28	29

SEP
01
SUN

♅ St ℞ ♉
Uranus Stations Retrograde in 27º Taurus

Toward every year end we can count on the retrogradation of Uranus, which makes us review all the technological advances we have made this past season. The work begins in earnest tomorrow!

♇ ℞ ♑
Pluto Retrograde goes back to Capricorn until 19 November

Can you believe that we will still have a final stretch of Pluto in Capricorn to contend with? This is when we receive all the blessings for having literally deconstructed massive old internal structures in our being. The world is completely different from 2008; we are in the New Age, where the collective forces are screaming for new transformations. Now is the time to release everything you still retain from the old world.

☽ ♌
Moon in Leo

SEP
02
MON

♅ ℞ ♉
Uranus Retrograde in Taurus until 30 January 2025

Between now and January don't schedule any major digital launches; just review and refine the plans you have for your social media, marketing campaigns and website. Buying new equipment should also wait.

☽ ♍
Moon in Virgo

S	M	T	W	T	F	S	S	M	T	W	T	F	S	S	M	T	W	T	F	S	S	M	T	W	T	F	S	S	M
1	2	3	4	5	6	7	8	9	10	11	12	13	14	15	16	17	18	19	20	21	22	23	24	25	26	27	28	29	30

רי
ה·ה·ו·י
Meditation for the month of Elul
Scan with your eyes from right to left

VIRGO

3 SEPTEMBER – 1:56AM (UTC) – NEW MOON 11° VIRGO

Los Angeles (UTC −7) • New York (UTC −4) • London (UTC +1)
Paris (UTC +2) • Sydney (UTC +11)

IN THE NEXT SIX MONTHS I WILL MANIFEST...

Organized routines Clean environments Efficiency Analysis	Patience Health checks Self-care Balancing control	Perception of details My body my rules Delicacy Forgiveness

SEP
03
TUE

♂ ♊ □ ♆ ♓
Mars in Gemini squares Neptune in Pisces

Confusion is in sight! Today is not a good day to make decisions or pursue a particular path. Major undertakings can diverge from the planned route and leave you unsure of what to do. Just wait a few days and, with a more focused mindset, you'll be better able to judge the situation.

● ♍
New Moon 11º Virgo

We begin the lunar month of Virgo, purifying our feelings and cleaning our spaces. In this season, we try our best to have a clean mind, body and spirit, so a nice detox would suit you very well. Practise careful fasting to achieve even greater visions, and talk to a nutritionist.

SEP
04
WED

♂ ♋
Mars enters Cancer until 4 November

An incomparable time to learn from past mistakes. A sudden change of mood can create imbalances in your relationships and put everything at risk. On the other hand, repressed anger could give you a stomach ache. Channel your energy by refining your care for yourself and your love. Gather in affection.

☽ ♎
Moon in Libra

SEP
05
THU

☽ ♎
Moon in Libra

SEP
06
FRI

☽ ♎
Moon in Libra

S	M	T	W	T	F	S	S	M	T	W	T	F	S	S	M	T	W	T	F	S	S	M	T	W	T	F	S	S	M
1	2	3	4	5	6	7	8	9	10	11	12	13	14	15	16	17	18	19	20	21	22	23	24	25	26	27	28	29	30

SEP
07
SAT

☿ ♌ □ ♅ ℞ ♉
Mercury in Leo squares Uranus Retrograde in Taurus

For the third time, we experience the same planetary conversation that took place on both 21 July and 18 August. Perhaps you are now more certain about what you do or do not want in your life, and where you wish to rule. Channel your energy into sharing your talents only with those who deserve them.

☽ ♏
Moon in Scorpio

SEP
08
SUN

☉ ♍ ☍ ♄ ℞ ♓
Sun in Virgo opposite Saturn Retrograde in Pisces

All the restrictions and care you have imposed on yourself lately are taking effect; you are prioritising your well-being and therefore deserve rest. Today's aspect makes you proud of the effort you made in the past. Enjoy!

☽ ♏
Moon in Scorpio

SEP
09
MON

☿ ♍
Mercury enters Virgo for the second time until 26 September

For the second time since 25 July, Mercury returns to his home in Virgo, and we are increasingly attached to our new routines. If you have met your own needs, now you are ready to move one stage further and think logically about how to achieve your goals in this coming season.

☽ ♐
Moon in Sagittarius

SEP
10
TUE

☽ ♐
Moon in Sagittarius

S	M	T	W	T	F	S	S	M	T	W	T	F	S	S	M	T	W	T	F	S	S	M	T	W	T	F	S	S	M
1	2	3	4	5	6	7	8	9	10	11	12	13	14	15	16	17	18	19	20	21	22	23	24	25	26	27	28	29	30

SEP
11
WED

◐ ♐
First Quarter 19º Sagittarius

Today's Waxing Crescent Moon helps you to adjust the aim of your arrow and hit the right target. Take a wider perspective so that you can see the whole picture. Time for action – good luck!

SEP
12
THU

☿ ♍ ⚹ ♂ ♋
Mercury in Virgo sextile Mars in Cancer

You have the mental energy necessary to sort through all your best ideas, but you may be missing the coolness and calmness needed to make the best decisions. The impulse is to do everything at once, but you know that nothing will come out perfect that way. Consistency and firmness are required to reach your dreams!

☉ ♍ □ ♃ ♊
Sun in Virgo square Jupiter in Gemini

Optimism presides over all situations, and you can be hopeful that this is an incredible moment for which you've been waiting a long time. Brimming with confidence, try not to risk too much, and don't attempt to grab every opportunity at the same time.

☽ ♑
Moon in Capricorn

SEP
13
FRI

☽ ♑
Moon in Capricorn

SEP
14
SAT

☽ ♒
Moon in Aquarius

SEP
15
SUN

♀ ♎ △ ♃ ♊
Venus in Libra trine Jupiter in Gemini

A Sunday of fun and celebration! We are finishing up a season and it's time to celebrate. Try to channel that excitement into other areas of life besides friendships; get stuck in, and you'll see luck and success coming your way.

☽ ♒
Moon in Aquarius

SEP
16
MON

☽ ♓
Moon in Pisces

S	M	T	W	T	F	S	S	M	T	W	T	F	S	S	M	T	W	T	F	S	S	M	T	W	T	F	S	S	M
1	2	3	4	5	6	7	8	9	10	11	12	13	**14**	**15**	16	17	18	19	20	**21**	**22**	23	24	25	26	27	**28**	**29**	30

SEP
17
TUE

☽ ♓
Moon in Pisces

SEP
18
WED

☿ ♍ ☍ ♄ ℞ ♓
Mercury in Virgo opposite Saturn Retrograde in Pisces

Yes, there are many demands on us at the moment, and we are super-focused on finishing our tasks. But we have a highly emotional Eclipse on the way, and some worries and regrets may arise. Take a deep breath!

○ ♓
Full Moon Partial Eclipse 25º Pisces

Physical and spiritual realities come together tonight. Celebrate your milestones from last year up until now, and how much emotional maturity you've achieved! Explore meditation, prayers and gratitude; be grateful for all you have faced and receive the blessings. This Eclipse is a radical shift in your spiritual connection.

SEP
19
THU

☉ ♍ △ ♅ ℞ ♉
Sun in Virgo trine Uranus Retrograde in Taurus

Right around the time of the Equinox, you may feel ready to finally make the necessary changes and let go of that extra emotional weight, to better balance your journey. Time to expand inward and grow your personality positively. Open yourself to new opportunities in this new season.

☽ ♈
Moon in Aries

SEP
20
FRI

☽ ♉
Moon in Taurus

S	M	T	W	T	F	S	S	M	T	W	T	F	S	S	M	T	W	T	F	S	S	M	T	W	T	F	S	S	M
1	2	3	4	5	6	**7**	**8**	9	10	11	12	13	**14**	**15**	16	17	18	19	20	**21**	**22**	23	24	25	26	27	**28**	**29**	30

SEP
21
SAT

☉ ♍ ☍ ♆ ℞ ♓
Sun in Virgo opposite Neptune Retrograde in Pisces

Saturday comes like a reality shock, as the Universe wants to know if you are dreaming or if you are firmly grounded. Dream big, but create the plans to bring those dreams into the world.

☿ ♍ □ ♃ ♊
Mercury in Virgo squares Jupiter in Gemini

It's a day of illusions for sure; maybe you're delighted with a new group of friends, or even very entertained with your new way of expressing yourself. Either way, be selective and only promise what you can deliver.

☽ ♉
Moon in Taurus

SEP
22
SUN

☉ ♍ △ ♇ ℞ ♑
Sun in Virgo trine Pluto Retrograde in Capricorn

Just before we tip into Libra, Pluto reminds you of your power to go for exactly what you want. Make contact with important people this coming Libra season.

☉ ♎
Sun enters Libra

Time to beautify the world, and seek balance between mind, body and spirit!.Seek partnerships that raise your potential, welcome people into your home, and avoid all kinds of conflict – even internal ones!

Fall Equinox - Mabon North Hemisphere
Spring Equinox - Ostara South Hemisphere

☽ ♊
Moon in Gemini

LIBRA

22 September / 12:44PM (UTC)

AIR VENUS

LIBRA

MODE Cardinal **ELEMENT** Air **RULING PLANET** Venus

CRYSTAL Sapphire **BACH FLOWER REMEDY** Scleranthus

PRINCIPLE Positive **OPPOSITE SIGN** Aries

LIBRA AND SIGNS IN LOVE

Aries	Libra
Taurus	Scorpio
Gemini	Sagittarius
Cancer	Capricorn
Leo	Aquarius
Virgo	Pisces

MANTRA I balance **POWER** Harmony

KEYWORD Relation **ANATOMY** Kidneys, Appendix, Lumbar, Adrenal glands

LIGHT
Cooperative
Persuasive
Refined
Impartial
Artistic
Diplomatic
Sociable

SHADOW
Fickle
Apathetic
Intriguing
Peace at any price
Grumpy
Undecided
Easily discouraged

SEP
23
MON

♀ ♏
Venus enters Scorpio until 17 October

We begin the week by diving deep into our most intimate and personal questions. Venus in Scorpio gets a little obsessed with past traumas, so look for ways to empty out your old baggage. Focus on something that gets your senses vibrating.

☽ ♊
Moon in Gemini

SEP
24
TUE

◑ ♋
Last Quarter 2º Cancer

This Moon makes you understand that very often what causes you imbalance is exactly the sorrow you crystallized in your heart long ago. Be gentle with your path but eliminate once and for all the resentment that prevents you from creating healthier relationships.

SEP
25
WED

☿ ♍ ☍ ♆ ℞ ♓
Mercury in Virgo opposite Neptune Retrograde in Pisces

It is not a good day for presentations as our mind is focused on details of our imagination. A good day to analyze how well you have been serving your purpose on Earth. It's also good for thinking up more creative methods of serving the world by attending to your talents.

☽ ♋
Moon in Cancer

SEP
26
THU

☿ ♍ △ ♇ ℞ ♑
Mercury in Virgo trine Pluto Retrograde in Capricorn

This influence puts you in a very favourable position, as suddenly people tell you their greatest secrets and you manage to convince them of your standing. Collect precious information but keep to yourself that which doesn't concern anyone else.

☿ ♎
Mercury enters Libra until 13 October

Now in Libra, Mercury will want to get justice. Maybe your privileged information has made you realize that there is something messing with your principles, and this makes you very uncomfortable. Try to take advantage of this transit to avoid getting into trouble.

☽ ♌
Moon in Leo

SEP
27
FRI

☽ ♌
Moon in Leo

SEP
28
SAT

☽ ♌
Moon in Leo

SEP
29
SUN

☽ ♍
Moon in Virgo

SEP
30
MON

♂ ♋ △ ♄ ℞ ♓
Mars in Cancer trine Saturn Retrograde in Pisces

Today brings you the confidence that a labour of love must be done with an keen eye for detail and this slows the process down. Continue steadily in your ongoing efforts to be a new person.

☉ ☌ ☿ ♎
Sun meets Mercury in Libra

A day to analyse all the things that are happening in your life. Your thinking is balanced and you make decisions based on your personal needs – perfect! Work on your speaking and writing skills.

☽ ♍
Moon in Virgo

OCTOBER

the first day of the month starts with the ephemeris

☉	8º	♎
☽	25º	♍
☿	8º	♎
♀	10º	♏
♂	15º	♋
♃	21º	♊
♄℞	14º	♓
♅℞	27º	♉
♆℞	28º	♓
♇℞	29º	♑

MON	TUE	WED
	01	02
07	08	09
14	15	16
21	22	23
28	29	30

THU	FRI	SAT	SUN
03	04	05	06
10	11	12	13
17	18	19	20
24	25	26	27
31			

OCT
01
TUE

☽ ♎
Moon in Libra

OCT
02
WED

● ♎
New Moon Annular Eclipse 10º Libra

The New Moon opens a new chapter in relationships today. How do you want to communicate with your partner from now on? Avoid the passive-aggressive vibe and learn to be even more assertive in how you communicate.

פל
ו·ה·י·ה
Meditation for the month of Tishrei
Scan with your eyes from right to left

L I B R A

ANNULAR ECLIPSE

2 OCTOBER - 6:49PM (UTC)
NEW MOON 10° LIBRA - ANNULAR ECLIPSE

Los Angeles (UTC −7) • New York (UTC −4) • London (UTC +1) • Paris (UTC +2) • Sydney (UTC +11)

IN THE NEXT SIX MONTHS I WILL MANIFEST...

Relationships
Partnerships
Commitment
Conciliation

Harmony
Perfectionism
Visual aesthetics
My own voice

My own opinions
Justice and honesty
Elegance
Charm

OCT
03
THU

☽ ♎
Moon in Libra

OCT
04
FRI

♀ ♏ △ ♄ ℞ ♓
Venus in Scorpio trine Saturn Retrograde in Pisces

Following gains in your career or studies, look at your finances and try to distance yourself from situations and people who drain your energy, whether physically, materially or mentally. Do the maths and see if the work involved is worth as much as your mental health. Relationships become even more solid and deep.

☽ ♏
Moon in Scorpio

OCT
05
SAT

☽ ♏
Moon in Scorpio

OCT
06
SUN

☿ ♎ □ ♂ ♋
Mercury in Libra squares Mars in Cancer

You may feel the urge to use your emotions to manipulate a situation, but while you know how good you are at convincing others, try not to do this by only focusing on your point of view. If you need to have a serious conversation, rehearse your speech and take action instead of saying something you may regret. Take it easy at this time!

☽ ♐
Moon in Sagittarius

OCT
07
MON

☽ ♐
Moon in Sagittarius

OCT
08
TUE

♀ ♏ △ ♂ ♋
Venus in Scorpio trine Mars in Cancer

Venus wants to play power games, while Mars just wants to snuggle up in a nurturing and loving nest. Relationships benefit if there is no tendency to take advantage of the weaknesses of others. New people can also enter your life and your heart, but watch out for overspending in an effort to impress.

☿ ♎ △ ♃ ♊
Mercury in Libra trine Jupiter in Gemini

Time to capitalize on your networking skills. It's very likely that among your group of friends are people who can help to increase your sources of funds and work! See who you can offer your talents to; your intellect knows exactly which door to knock on.

☽ ♐
Moon in Sagittarius

OCT
09
WED

♃ St ℞ ♊
Jupiter Stations Retrograde in 21º Gemini

We are preparing for internal growth over the next four months. Are you ready to increase your networking even more?

☽ ♑
Moon in Capricorn

OCT
10
THU

♃ ℞ ♊
Jupiter Retrograde in Gemini until 4 February 2025

Jupiter retrograding along with a Waxing Moon in Capricorn tells you that professional growth will come through hard work involving a group of friends. What is the source of self-esteem that supports your inner structures of selfhood?

◐ ♑
First Quarter 17º Capricorn

Time to strengthen your inner configurations and devote more of yourself to the construction of your dreams. Look for systems that help make your life easier, such as wellness apps, calendars and reminders that support you in getting things done.

OCT
11
FRI

☽ ♒
Moon in Aquarius

OCT
12
SAT

♇ St D ♑
Pluto Stations Direct in 29º Capricorn

As some leave, others return to shake things up with powerful vibes. This is the last time Pluto will transit Capricorn in your lifetime. He is about destroying that which no longer has any use, in order to shape something totally new and impressive. Look at the areas of life linked with Capricorn and feel the revolution coming!

☽ ♒
Moon in Aquarius

OCT
13
SUN

♇ D ♑
Pluto Direct in Capricorn until 19 November

Just over a month to go until we receive the gifts of this long season of Pluto in Capricorn. There have been 16 years of dismantling everything that was traditional and rigid, built by our ancestors. Now we are ready to innovate and live our freedom!

☿ ♎ □ ♇ ♑
Mercury in Libra squares Pluto in Capricorn

Before plunging into Scorpio, Mercury demonstrates his powers of persuasion once more. Your thoughts grow more honest each day, and you can trust that you are making your best impression on the world.

☿ ♏
Mercury enters Scorpio until 2 November

Be careful not to become completely devoted to one subject or area of your life and forget the others. This is the best time to seek therapy or a specialist to help you go deep into your healing process.

☽ ♓
Moon in Pisces

OCT
14
MON

☉ ♎ △ ♃ ℞ ♊
Sun in Libra trine Jupiter Retrograde in Gemini

This is the week in which you decide to bring justice into the work space or arena of your personal life. Perhaps you are feeling unfairly treated by friends or even your partner. Try to work on this within yourself first, before exposing the situation to everyone else.

☉ ♎ □ ♂ ♋
Sun in Libra squares Mars in Cancer

The feeling of unfairness could lead you to commit some emotional blackmail. It's a very delicate day with energy that could give you a shock. Be on your guard!

♀ ♏ ☍ ♅ ℞ ♉
Venus in Scorpio opposite Uranus Retrograde in Taurus

With this aspect, there is a strong desire to end any relationships that trigger you or that seem toxic, and to throw yourself into the unknown and start again from scratch. Stormy passions are running wild, but maybe you're just repeating old patterns? Take a moment to observe.

☽ ♓
Moon in Pisces

OCT
15
TUE

☽ ♈
Moon in Aries

OCT
16
WED

♀ ♏ △ ♆ ℞ ♓
Venus in Scorpio trine Neptune Retrograde in Pisces

After the storm, you seem much more willing and available for healthy relationships. With your partner, or with a relationship that has just begun, deepen your romantic connection, take advantage of the Moon in Aries and live out a romance in which you are the protagonist.

☽ ♈
Moon in Aries

T	W	T	F	S	S	M	T	W	T	F	S	S	M	T	W	T	F	S	S	M	T	W	T	F	S	S	M	T	W	T
1	2	3	4	**5**	**6**	7	8	9	10	11	**12**	**13**	14	15	16	17	18	**19**	**20**	21	22	23	24	25	**26**	**27**	28	29	30	31

OCT
17
THU

♀ ♏ ✱ ♇ ♑

Venus in Scorpio sextile Pluto in Capricorn

A great day for helping you achieve everything you desire. An extremely powerful Venus wants and will attract money and love if you make the right investment. Just watch who you invest your diamonds in.

♀ ♐

Venus enters Sagittarius until 11 November

Good humour shows signs of wanting to return, and we will have almost a month of adventures ahead of us. In finances, keep a more conservative outlook than before, and try not to overspend.

○ ♈

Full Moon 24º Aries

Time to create the ultimate inner balance sheet, and look at the gains you have won for yourself this year. Go back over the last 12 months and see how clear you are about what you want for yourself. Where is there room for more personal growth?

OCT
18
FRI

☽ ♉

Moon in Taurus

OCT
19
SAT

☽ ♊
Moon in Gemini

OCT
20
SUN

☽ ♊
Moon in Gemini

OCT
21
MON

☽ ♋
Moon in Cancer

OCT
22
TUE

☿ ♏ △ ♄ ℞ ♓
Mercury in Scorpio trine Saturn Retrograde in Pisces

A very important day to calculate risks and plan for your next goals. Today you have the necessary focus and concentration on your side to organize matters with all the excellence your dreams deserve.

☉ ♎ □ ♇ ♑
Sun in Libra squares Pluto in Capricorn

You could be giving up on your desires in order to avoid conflict, so feel disconnected in a relationship, which isn't fair! Use this aspect to stand out and focus on your self-care and beauty.

☉ ♏
Sun enters Scorpio

The Sun dips into deep Scorpio waters, and you feel even more intense. Time to discover the truth about your feelings and emotions and no longer be drawn into other people's desires. Go wherever you want and desire to go.

☽ ♋
Moon in Cancer

SCORPIO

22 October / 10:15PM (UTC)

SCORPIO

MODE Fixed **ELEMENT** Water **RULING PLANET** Pluto

CRYSTAL Tourmaline **BACH FLOWER REMEDY** Chicory

PRINCIPLE Negative **OPPOSITE SIGN** Taurus

SCORPIO AND SIGNS IN LOVE

Aries	♥ ♥ ♥ ♥ ♡	Libra	♥ ♡ ♡ ♡ ♡
Taurus	♥ ♥ ♥ ♥ ♥	Scorpio	♥ ♥ ♥ ♡ ♡
Gemini	♥ ♡ ♡ ♡ ♡	Sagittarius	♥ ♥ ♡ ♡ ♡
Cancer	♥ ♥ ♥ ♥ ♡	Capricorn	♥ ♥ ♥ ♡ ♡
Leo	♥ ♡ ♡ ♡ ♡	Aquarius	♥ ♥ ♡ ♡ ♡
Virgo	♥ ♥ ♥ ♥ ♡	Pisces	♥ ♥ ♥ ♥ ♥

MANTRA I desire **POWER** Intensity

ANATOMY Reproductive system, Sexual organs, Bladder

LIGHT
Motivated
Penetrating
Director
Determined
Scientific exploratory
Researcher
Passionate
Conscious

SHADOW
Vengeful
Temperamental
Reticent
Arrogant
Sarcastic
Suspicious
Jealous
Intolerant

OCT
23
WED

☽ ♋
Moon in Cancer

OCT
24
THU

◑ ♌
Last Quarter 1º Leo

Have fun eliminating from your life any superficial situations that don't value you in the way that you deserve. Sever at the root, smiling at what is bad for you. An excellent time to start analysing your emotions with a specialist.

OCT
25
FRI

♂ ♋ ✱ ♅ ℞ ♉
Mars in Cancer sextile Uranus Retrograde in Taurus

Involve your soul family to bring even more love and value into your work. Be among friends and remember situations in which you played an important part. Accept recognition for your role in the development of those around you. Your energy is vital for them, believe me!

☽ ♌
Moon in Leo

OCT
26
SAT

☽ ♍
Moon in Virgo

T	W	T	F	S	S	M	T	W	T	F	S	S	M	T	W	T	F	S	S	M	T	W	T	F	S	S	M	T	W	T
1	2	3	4	5	6	7	8	9	10	11	12	13	14	15	16	17	18	19	20	21	22	23	24	25	26	27	28	29	30	31

OCT
27
SUN

☽ ♍
Moon in Virgo

OCT
28
MON

♂ ♋ △ ♆ ℞ ♓
Mars in Cancer trine Neptune Retrograde in Pisces

You are able to help your family and friends even more, but you must learn to deal with the constructive criticism they give you. Or at least try to see all sides of a situation. With your charm and intuition sharpened, take the opportunity to conquer even more of what you want.

♀ ♐ □ ♄ ℞ ♓
Venus in Sagittarius squares Saturn Retrograde in Pisces

Don't waste your time discussing your dreams with your family. Be smart and let people explain their side of things, and listen so you can at least understand part of what may be bothering others. Being free from others' opinions comes at a cost.

☽ ♍
Moon in Virgo

OCT
29
TUE

☽ ♎
Moon in Libra

OCT
30
WED

☿ ♏ ☍ ♅ ℞ ♉
Mercury in Scorpio opposite Uranus Retrograde in Taurus

You know exactly how to spread your message and show your value to the whole collective. Be careful not to exclude those who do not yet see your potential, but who cheer for your success anyway. Work on trusting your instincts, as this is your best tool for growth.

☽ ♎
Moon in Libra

OCT
31
THU

☽ ♏
Moon in Scorpio

NO VEM BER

the first day of the month starts with the ephemeris

☉	9º	♏
☽	9º	♏
☿	28º	♏
♀	17º	♐
♂	29º	♋
♃℞	20º	♊
♄℞	13º	♓
♅℞	26º	♉
♆℞	27º	♓
♇	29º	♑

MON	TUE	WED
04	05	06
11	12	13
18	19	20
25	26	27

THU	FRI	SAT	SUN
	01	02	03
07	08	09	10
14	15	16	17
21	22	23	24
28	29	30	

NOV
01
FRI

☿ ♏ △ ♆ ℞ ♓
Mercury in Scorpio trine Neptune Retrograde in Pisces

Another very intense and magnetic Friday. Do you know to what extent you are attracting what you want in your life? Have you been trusting your powers of manifestation lately? Time to make your reality even more enchanted.

● ♏
New Moon 9º Scorpio

Tonight, define your intentions in terms of radical transformations in your life. In what area of life do you wish to radically change? What is the great transition that you will work on accomplishing in the next six months? Are you still attached to old feelings? Time to surrender and let go.

NOV
02
SAT

☿ ♏ △ ♂ ♋
Mercury in Scorpio trine Mars in Cancer

It's Saturday, but who wants a break? I want you to be working on your financial plan for next year. Today is a great day to research how to achieve your dream income in your bank account.

☿ ♏ ✱ ♇ ♑
Mercury in Scorpio sextile Pluto in Capricorn

At the same time, it would be really nice to have inspiring conversations with people who have already got where you aim to be. A good day for presentations, meetings and everything that concerns your future.

☿ ♐
Mercury enters Sagittarius until 8 January 2025 (will retrograde)

After so much intensity, a professional event may reach a golden conclusion. The excitement is such – especially since you have a thousand ideas to monetize – that you may find yourself talking about work even in your moments of rest. Try not to be too sincere.

☽ ♏
Moon in Scorpio

דנ
ו·ה·ה·י
Meditation for the month of Cheshvan
Scan with your eyes from right to left

SCORPIO

1 NOVEMBER – 12:47PM (UTC) – NEW MOON 9° SCORPIO

Los Angeles (UTC –7) • New York (UTC –4) • London (UTC +0) • Paris (UTC +1) • Sydney (UTC +12)

IN THE NEXT SIX MONTHS I WILL MANIFEST...

Intensity Transformation Magnetism End of cycle	Empowerment Hidden places Sexuality Ability to keep secrets	Surrender Deep unconscious Transmutation Rebirth

NOV
03
SUN

♂ ♋ ☍ ♇ ♑
Mars in Cancer opposite Pluto in Capricorn

Positive passions take you to the top of the mountain, but beware of dangerous activities and places today. Hang out with friends and don't be so stubborn about accepting the ideas of others.

♀ ♐ ☍ ♃ ℞ ♊
Venus in Sagittarius opposite Jupiter Retrograde in Gemini

Control the tendency to excess, especially if you are partying among friends. Too much drink and too much sincerity are not the best combination at this moment. Games of seduction can also cost you some laughs. Do everything with moderation.

☽ ♐
Moon in Sagittarius

NOV
04
MON

♂ ♌
Mars enters Leo until 6 January

Monday begins with the intensity of Mars rising in the sign of Leo. Now the party is ready! Your vision increases in magnitude and everything seems splendid in your self-confidence. The retrogradation will bring you the missing elements.

☉ ♏ △ ♄ ℞ ♓
Sun in Scorpio trine Saturn Retrograde in Pisces

It's possible that some past effort will start to be appreciated now. Be happy with the direction you've been taking on your journey, and feel joyful about the path you've decided to take and your responsibilities. Be generous, but don't take responsibility for what isn't yours.

☽ ♐
Moon in Sagittarius

NOV
05
TUE

☽ ♑
Moon in Capricorn

NOV
06
WED

☽ ♑
Moon in Capricorn

F	S	S	M	T	W	T	F	S	S	M	T	W	T	F	S	S	M	T	W	T	F	S	S	M	T	W	T	F	S
1	**2**	**3**	4	5	6	7	8	**9**	**10**	11	12	13	14	15	**16**	**17**	18	19	20	21	22	**23**	**24**	25	26	27	28	29	**30**

NOV
07
THU

☽ ♒
Moon in Aquarius

NOV
08
FRI

☽ ♒
Moon in Aquarius

F	S	S	M	T	W	T	F	S	S	M	T	W	T	F	S	S	M	T	W	T	F	S	S	M	T	W	T	F	S
1	**2**	**3**	4	5	6	7	8	**9**	**10**	11	12	13	14	15	**16**	**17**	18	19	20	21	22	**23**	**24**	25	26	27	28	29	**30**

NOV
09
SAT

♀ ♐ □ ♆ ♓
Venus in Sagittarius squares Neptune in Pisces

A Friday of romance at its highest! Emotions run riot and it's easy to get lost in the ideal fantasy. Just ask yourself whether you are in love with the person or the idea of falling in love. At work, this is not the time to hire anyone new, as we are all much too far removed from reality for that.

First Quarter 17º Aquarius

Look at all the small transformations that you have accomplished in your life lately and feel a surge of surprise around new ways of seeing yourself and living. Step out of your comfort zone a little more to experience the changes on other levels.

NOV
10
SUN

☽ ♓
Moon in Pisces

F	**S**	**S**	M	T	W	T	F	**S**	**S**	M	T	W	T	F	**S**	**S**	M	T	W	T	F	**S**	**S**	M	T	W	T	F	**S**
1	**2**	**3**	4	5	6	7	8	**9**	**10**	11	12	13	14	15	**16**	**17**	18	19	20	21	22	**23**	**24**	25	26	27	28	29	**30**

NOV
11
MON

♀ ♑

Venus enters Capricorn until 7 December

This entrance of Venus into Capricorn brings our desires down to Earth. Insecurity may shake your plans, and the fear of rejection saps your confidence. Make sure your worries haven't distorted your focus and you're not overly concerned with material fulfilment rather than enjoying the process.

☽ ♓

Moon in Pisces

NOV
12
TUE

☿ ♐ □ ♄ ℞ ♓

Mercury in Sagittarius squares Saturn Retrograde in Pisces

Another aspect that brings regrets and worries. In this week when Saturn wakes up, be aware of the responsibilities you need to take on now. Your to-do list may be huge, but focus on being organized and keep thinking positively about the future.

☽ ♈

Moon in Aries

NOV
13
WED

☽ ♈
Moon in Aries

NOV
14
THU

☽ ♉
Moon in Taurus

NOV
15
FRI

♄ St D ♓
Saturn Stations Direct in 12º Pisces

Saturn is preparing to get back on track just in time for this Full Moon, when we shine a light on all the changes in our values that have brought us even more self-esteem.

○ ♉
Full Moon 24º Taurus

Celebrate how important it was for you to let go of low-vibration feelings in order to boost your confidence. What are the emotions that really align with your beliefs? What brings you emotional security? Show that you trust your instincts.

NOV
16
SAT

♄ D ♓
Saturn Direct in Pisces

We have had almost five months of re-evaluating our commitments and responsibilities. Saturn Direct now asks you to feel even more secure in following your heart and fulfilling your dreams. By making all the necessary adjustments and placing boundaries along the way, you will go far.

☽ ♊
Moon in Gemini

NOV
17
SUN

☉ ♏ ☍ ♅ ℞ ♉
Sun in Scorpio opposite Uranus Retrograde in Taurus

Ready or not, this Sun asks you to analyse the value of each change you have made to your own story. Give yourself a score for your finances in the past year and now. This is a day to go even deeper into studying how to honour your values.

☽ ♊
Moon in Gemini

NOV
18
MON

☿ ♐ ☍ ♃ ℞ ♊
Mercury in Sagittarius opposite Jupiter Retrograde in Gemini

You have a great message to share, and you are optimistic about revealing its light to the world, but watch the deadline you have set yourself for this manifestation and be aware that it will not transpire exactly as you may have predicted. Don't overbook your appointments, or you may have to cancel some last-minute meetings this week.

☽ ♋
Moon in Cancer

NOV
19
TUE

☉ ♏ △ ♆ ℞ ♓
Sun in Scorpio trine Neptune Retrograde in Pisces

Your sensitivity can be your greatest ally in the manifestation of your new reality. Today is a great day to tune in even more to your spirit guides and guardian angels, and visualize the future you want to experience in the coming years.

♇ ♒
Pluto enters Aquarius until 9 March 2043

The definitive entrance of Pluto into Aquarius is the sign from the Universe that was previously lacking, asking you to look even more closely into this area of your life. Make a Dream Wall, a vision board where you express all your greatest and most ambitious wishes for the next 19 years! Open a portal in the sky and plant your boldest seeds.

☽ ♋
Moon in Cancer

NOV
20
WED

☽ ♌
Moon in Leo

NOV
21
THU

☉ ♐
Sun enters Sagittarius

As if the week were not intense enough, the Sun climbs on the back of the centaur Sagittarius for the final ride of this chapter. Your arrows will soar as high as your mind can imagine, so aim to launch them far and wide!

☉ ♐ ⚹ ♇ ♒
Sun in Sagittarius sextile Pluto in Aquarius

Already in this first meeting, Pluto wants to bring us an expansion of collective consciousness. We may all be going through the same doubts, which indicates that certain structures are not strong enough and deserve to be reconsidered. Place all your focus on visualizing a new horizon!

☽ ♌
Moon in Leo

NOV
22
FRI

♀ ♑ ⚹ ♄ ♓
Venus in Capricorn sextile Saturn in Pisces

An excellent conversation between Venus and Saturn in such a special week. We can separate out those people and situations that are holding back our advancement in life and everything else that is vibrating with an individual consciousness. Stick to the good ones!

☽ ♍
Moon in Virgo

SAGITTARIUS

21 November / 7:56PM (UTC)

△ ♃

FIRE JUPITER

SAGITTARIUS

MODE Mutable **ELEMENT** Fire **RULING PLANET** Jupiter

CRYSTAL Citrine **BACH FLOWER REMEDY** Agrimony

PRINCIPLE Positive **OPPOSITE SIGN** Gemini

SAGITTARIUS AND SIGNS IN LOVE

Aries	♥ ♥ ♥ ♥ ♥	Libra	♥ ♥ ♡ ♡ ♡
Taurus	♥ ♥ ♡ ♡ ♡	Scorpio	♥ ♥ ♥ ♡ ♡
Gemini	♥ ♥ ♥ ♥ ♡	Sagittarius	♥ ♥ ♥ ♥ ♡
Cancer	♥ ♡ ♡ ♡ ♡	Capricorn	♥ ♥ ♡ ♡ ♡
Leo	♥ ♥ ♥ ♥ ♥	Aquarius	♥ ♥ ♥ ♥ ♡
Virgo	♥ ♡ ♡ ♡ ♡	Pisces	♥ ♥ ♥ ♡ ♡

MANTRA I understand **POWER** Visualization

KEYWORD Explore **ANATOMY** Hips, Thighs, Upper legs

LIGHT

Honest
Philosophical
Free lover
Athletic
Generous
Optimistic
Fair
Enthusiastic

SHADOW

Inclined to discussions
Exaggerated
Chatty
Procrastinator
Self-indulgent
Brash
Impatient
Player

NOV
23
SAT

Last Quarter 1º Virgo

Now that you are determined to move away from low vibrations and dirty energy, it's time now to be practical and eliminate anything that is contaminated with the past and with misconceptions. Holding on to all those things is restricting you from feeling the confidence that this moment begs for. Make space for new intentions.

NOV
24
SUN

☽ ♍

Moon in Virgo

NOV
25
MON

☽ ♎
Moon in Libra

NOV
26
TUE

☿ St ℞ ♐
Mercury Stations Retrograde in 22º Sagittarius

The quantum shift we are making demands an upgrade in our mental software as well. Mercury now finds that some truths no longer touch his heart, and are becoming outdated. We will begin to develop a new lifestyle tomorrow.

☽ ♎
Moon in Libra

NOV
27
WED

☿ ℞ ♐
Mercury Retrograde in Sagittarius until 15 December

Only 18 days remain to upgrade our minds to a new intellectual level, up to date and ready to be used. Intuitive flashes of truth may threaten to dissipate your mental strength. Write it all down to reach some conclusions.

☉ ♐ △ ♂ ♌
Sun in Sagittarius trine Mars in Leo

We begin a highly energetic and dynamic phase. You move quickly in your mission and success is almost guaranteed. Just be careful not to overload yourself, as we cannot count on Mercury in the coming days. Aim for a more sustainable and less accelerated rhythm. Be confident!

☽ ♎
Moon in Libra

NOV
28
THU

☽ ♏
Moon in Scorpio

F	**S**	**S**	M	T	W	T	F	**S**	**S**	M	T	W	T	F	**S**	**S**	M	T	W	T	F	**S**	**S**	M	T	W	T	F	**S**
1	**2**	**3**	4	5	6	7	8	**9**	**10**	11	12	13	14	15	**16**	**17**	18	19	20	21	22	**23**	**24**	25	26	27	28	29	**30**

NOV
29
FRI

☽ ♏
Moon in Scorpio

NOV
30
SAT

☽ ♐
Moon in Sagittarius

F	S	S	M	T	W	T	F	S	S	M	T	W	T	F	S	S	M	T	W	T	F	S	S	M	T	W	T	F	S
1	**2**	**3**	4	5	6	7	8	**9**	**10**	11	12	13	14	15	**16**	**17**	18	19	20	21	22	**23**	**24**	25	26	27	28	29	**30**

DECEMBER

the first day of the month starts with the ephemeris

☉	9º	♐
☽	12º	♐
☿℞	21º	♐
♀	23º	♑
♂	6º	♌
♃℞	17º	♊
♄	13º	♓
♅℞	25º	♉
♆℞	27º	♓
♇	0º	♒

MON	TUE	WED
02	03	04
09	10	11
16	17	18
23	24	25
30	31	

THU	FRI	SAT	SUN
			01
05	06	07	08
12	13	14	15
19	20	21	22
26	27	28	29

DEC
01
SUN

New Moon 9º Sagittarius

A wonderful opportunity to set new goals for how you explore the world and receive divine inspiration. It's everything you've been waiting for when it comes to developing a new philosophy and experiencing new universes through travel, teaching and learning. Write down here the best motivational phrases or quotes that have inspired you lately.

DEC
02
MON

♀ ♑ △ ♅ ℞ ♉

Venus in Capricorn trine Uranus Retrograde in Taurus

Get close to the right people at work and surround yourself with your dream team. Teamwork flows really well, and this can be a favourable financial period. Especially favourable for freelancers, as you can plan exactly who you want to work for from now on.

☽ ♑

Moon in Capricorn

S	M	T	W	T	F	S	S	M	T	W	T	F	S	S	M	T	W	T	F	S	S	M	T	W	T	F	S	S	M	T
1	2	3	4	5	6	**7**	**8**	9	10	11	12	13	**14**	**15**	16	17	18	19	20	**21**	**22**	23	24	25	26	27	**28**	**29**	30	31

סג
ה·י·ה·ו
Meditation for the month of Kislev
Scan with your eyes from right to left

S A G I T T A R I U S

1 DECEMBER - 6:21AM (UTC) - NEW MOON 9° SAGITTARIUS

Los Angeles (UTC –8) • New York (UTC –5) • London (UTC +0)
Paris (UTC +1) • Sydney (UTC +12)

IN THE NEXT SIX MONTHS I WILL MANIFEST...

Global exploration New directions Freedom Optimism	Spontaneity Search for truth Physical exercises Overkill	Long studies Investigation Philosophy Foreign cultures

DEC
03
TUE

☽ ♑
Moon in Capricorn

DEC
04
WED

☿ ℞ ♐ ☍ ♃ ℞ ♊
Mercury Retrograde in Sagittarius opposite Jupiter Retrograde in Gemini

The same planetary conversation as on 18 November, so revisit your core message but without the illusion that you control everything. Reconsider various opinions and/or what your team expects from you. Commit yourself to doing fewer tasks this week and don't overstretch yourself.

☉ ♐ □ ♄ ♓
Sun in Sagittarius squares Saturn in Pisces

You will get what you deserve according to your past actions, but you believe that in order to get it done, you need to do it all by yourself. Divide up the responsibilities with those involved in each project, and only do your part. Limit yourself to what is yours.

♀ ♑ ⚹ ♆ ℞ ♓
Venus in Capricorn sextile Neptune Retrograde in Pisces

Release the emotions you've been repressing lately. Bring more sensuality into your life and reward yourself by acquiring something that makes you feel even more powerful.

☽ ♑
Moon in Capricorn

DEC
05
THU

☽ ♒
Moon in Aquarius

DEC
06
FRI

☉ ☌ ☿ ℞ ♐
Sun meets Mercury Retrograde in Sagittarius

At the midpoint of the retrogradation, it's time to start practising our new truth; a new way of living is trying to become reality. Strengthen your convictions by sharing them with those closest to you, and add anything that seems reasonable to you. Define your authenticity even more strongly.

♂ St ℞ ♌
Mars Stations Retrograde in 6º Leo

Mars in Leo is pure fun, but you can be overly self-centred and ride roughshod over the wishes of others. Time to review your actions and readjust your course to harness even more of your originality.

☿ ℞ ♐ □ ♄ ♓
Mercury Retrograde in Sagittarius squares Saturn in Pisces

Mercury retrograde regrets taking on so many commitments. Be responsible and wait until next week to give up anything that doesn't belong to you.

☽ ♒
Moon in Aquarius

DEC
07
SAT

♀ ♒
Venus enters Aquarius until 3 January

Venus wants to release you from all that restrains you and for you to live according to your own rules, without caring who may accept them or not. It's the shout of self-approval that you needed.

♀ ☌ ♇ ♒
Venus meets Pluto in Aquarius

Venus has barely entered and has already run into Pluto, who throws at her the responsibility to think of new laws that can serve not only the individual but also the entire group. Venus wants to test new technologies, and Pluto guarantees that power now lies in being eccentric. Take risks!

☉ ♐ ☍ ♃ ℞ ♊
Sun in Sagittarius opposite Jupiter Retrograde in Gemini

Happiness is knocking on your door, and it's time to develop a new way of looking at life. Grab every opportunity to spread your message in a bigger scope.

♂ ℞ ♌
Mars Retrograde in Leo until 23 February 2025

Your actions are no longer enough on their own; join with others to strengthen your creativity.

☽ ♓
Moon in Pisces

DEC
08
SUN

♆ D ♓
Neptune Direct in Pisces

A Sunday of great faith and benevolence, today your heart expands and you smile again at the future. It's been a very challenging few months, but you've weathered them all, and you've navigated them well, even through the storms. Celebrate your faith!

◐ ♓
First Quarter 17º Pisces

Check with your intuition which actions are most recommended from now on. We are all more vibrant and enlightened and even more connected to our spirituality. Connect with your soul deep inside today!

DEC
09
MON

☽ ♈
Moon in Aries

DEC
10
TUE

☽ ♈
Moon in Aries

S	M	T	W	T	F	S	S	M	T	W	T	F	S	S	M	T	W	T	F	S	S	M	T	W	T	F	S	S	M	T
1	2	3	4	5	6	**7**	**8**	9	10	11	12	13	**14**	**15**	16	17	18	19	20	**21**	**22**	23	24	25	26	27	**28**	**29**	30	31

DEC
11
WED

☽ ♉
Moon in Taurus

DEC
12
THU

♀ ♒ ☍ ♂ ℞ ♌
Venus in Aquarius opposite Mars Retrograde in Leo

Your ideas attract people, and you can feel the sparks in the air with certain folks. There is a strong attraction; however, it seems to be more mental and physical, and that's OK for those who don't want something long-lasting. Enjoy the moment without worrying too much or creating misunderstandings.

☽ ♉
Moon in Taurus

DEC
13
FRI

☿ ℞ ♐ ✱ ♀ ♒
Mercury Retrograde in Sagittarius sextile Venus in Aquarius

Before waking up and stationing direct, Mercury reminds your best friend of their emotional responsibility, not to be so forward thinking and to take into account their freedom and the feelings of others. Communicate with them and come to a mutual agreement.

☽ ♊
Moon in Gemini

DEC
14
SAT

☽ ♊
Moon in Gemini

S	M	T	W	T	F	S	S	M	T	W	T	F	S	S	M	T	W	T	F	S	S	M	T	W	T	F	S	S	M	T
1	2	3	4	5	6	**7**	**8**	9	10	11	12	13	**14**	**15**	16	17	18	19	20	**21**	**22**	23	24	25	26	27	**28**	**29**	30	31

DEC
15
SUN

☿ St D ♐
Mercury Stations Direct in 6º Sagittarius

Mercury wakes up to celebrate the Full Moon in his house, and we can already celebrate with a new awareness. The wisdom gained in recent months is taken on board and becomes part of your message.

○ ♊
Full Moon 23º Gemini

Time to spread your new theories, purpose of life and ideology with your friends. Since June this year, consider how your sense of freedom has given you even more knowledge. Express yourself in words, writing down all those thoughts in the pages of this diary. Welcome fresh insights.

DEC
16
MON

☿ D ♐
Mercury Direct in Sagittarius

In the last full business week of the year for many, you may want to settle everything in a few days' time. Organize paperwork, provide and approve all the actions that were a little confused earlier this month and take action in your life – sign, direct, delegate.

☽ ♋
Moon in Cancer

DEC
17
TUE

☽ ♌︎
Moon in Leo

DEC
18
WED

☉ ♐︎ □ ♆ ♓︎
Sun in Sagittarius squares Neptune in Pisces

Your head has already made up your mind, but your spirit seems to insist on walking in the clouds. Take advantage of the insights of this connection, listen more to your intuition and get fully in touch with your spirituality. Meditate!

☽ ♌︎
Moon in Leo

DEC
19
THU

☽ ♌
Moon in Leo

DEC
20
FRI

♀ ♒ △ ♃ ℞ ♊
Venus in Aquarius trine Jupiter Retrograde in Gemini

We are ready to socialize and attend as many different events as possible. Talk about your manifestations and inspire others to follow in your footsteps. Have fun!

☽ ♍
Moon in Virgo

DEC
21
SAT

☉ ♑
Sun enters Capricorn

It's the Solstice – showing that it is time to dedicate yourself even more to your mission of Life on Earth. A great time to share your blessings with the world and to perform acts of charity and kindness; you now have the disposition to build the future you so desire. Increase your self-esteem by honouring your victories.

Winter Solstice - Yule North Hemisphere
Summer Solstice - Litha South Hemisphere

☽ ♍
Moon in Virgo

DEC
22
SUN

◑ ♎
Last Quarter 1º Libra

The best moment to release anything that is stealing the energy you need to reach your true objectives. Any unbalanced relationships will tend to end now. Look at who you are with during the holidays.

CAPRICORN

21 December / 09:20AM (UTC)

CAPRICORN

MODE Cardinal **ELEMENT** Earth **RULING SIGN** Saturn

CRYSTAL Turquoise **BACH FLOWER REMEDY** Mimulus

PRINCIPLE Negative **OPPOSITE SIGN** Cancer

CAPRICORN AND SIGNS IN LOVE

Aries	♥ ♡ ♡ ♡ ♡	Libra	♥ ♥ ♥ ♡ ♡
Taurus	♥ ♥ ♥ ♥ ♥	Scorpio	♥ ♥ ♡ ♡ ♡
Gemini	♥ ♥ ♡ ♡ ♡	Sagittarius	♥ ♡ ♡ ♡ ♡
Cancer	♥ ♥ ♥ ♥ ♡	Capricorn	♥ ♥ ♥ ♡ ♡
Leo	♥ ♥ ♡ ♡ ♡	Aquarius	♥ ♥ ♡ ♡ ♡
Virgo	♥ ♥ ♥ ♥ ♥	Pisces	♥ ♥ ♥ ♡ ♡

MANTRA I know **POWER** Vision

KEYWORD Imagination **ANATOMY** Knees, Bones and Teeth

LIGHT

Cautious
Responsible
Scrupulous
Professional
Traditional
Practical
Economical
Serious worker

SHADOW

Selfish
Dominating
Spiteful
Fatalistic
Conventional
Stubborn
Inhibited
Searching for status

DEC
23
MON

☽ ♎
Moon in Libra

DEC
24
TUE

♃ ℞ ♊ □ ♄ ♓
Jupiter Retrograde in Gemini squares Saturn in Pisces

Don't overload yourself with party tasks – don't invite too many people to your celebrations, or, if you do, delegate roles to guests so that you don't have to deal with all the preparations. Learn to say no if you want to enjoy your achievements of this past year; spend time only with those who respect your limits.

☽ ♎
Moon in Libra

DEC
25
WED

☽ ♏
Moon in Scorpio

DEC
26
THU

☿ ♐ ☍ ♃ ℞ ♊
Mercury in Sagittarius opposite Jupiter Retrograde in Gemini (for the third time: 18 November–4 December)

We have no control over anything, and it could be that a lack of boundaries has drained you of all your energy. Go back to the days when this planetary conversation last took place to get even more clues.

☽ ♏
Moon in Scorpio

DEC
27
FRI

☿ ♐ □ ♄ ♓
Mercury in Sagittarius squares Saturn in Pisces
(for the third time: 12 November–7 December)

You may go back on some decision you made, or even not commit to something you'd promised in the last few months. Don't force yourself to keep your word if you know others involved would act differently.

☽ ♐
Moon in Sagittarius

DEC
28
SAT

♀ ♒ □ ♅ ℞ ♉
Venus in Aquarius squares Uranus Retrograde in Taurus

Again, there is a desire for new relationships and a need for independence within them. Those friendships that first arrived like a bolt of lightning bring the dose of fun and freshness you so desperately seek. More relaxed friendships take over your life now!

☽ ♐
Moon in Sagittarius

DEC
29
SUN

☽ ♐
Moon in Sagittarius

DEC
30
MON

● ♑
New Moon 9º Capricorn

Before the New Year, this New Moon invites you not only to determine your professional goals for the approaching season but also how you wish to feel emotionally about these upcoming steps. What feelings do you want to experience in your career in 2025? What are the goals you want to achieve in your professional and personal life in this coming year? Answer with your heart and be happy!

S	M	T	W	T	F	S	S	M	T	W	T	F	S	S	M	T	W	T	F	S	S	M	T	W	T	F	S	S	M	T
1	2	3	4	5	6	**7**	**8**	9	10	11	12	13	**14**	**15**	16	17	18	19	20	**21**	**22**	23	24	25	26	27	**28**	**29**	30	31

עב
ה·י·ה·ו
Meditation for the month of Tevet
Scan with your eyes from right to left

C A P R I C O R N

30 DECEMBER - 10:27PM (UTC) - NEW MOON 10° CAPRICORN

Los Angeles (UTC −8) • New York (UTC −5) • London (UTC +0) • Paris (UTC +1) • Sydney (UTC +11)

IN THE NEXT SIX MONTHS I WILL MANIFEST...

Security
Ambition
Social status
Career

Long-term goals
Recognition
Planning
Financial stability

High states of being
Merit
Reward
Hard work

DEC
31
TUE

☽ ♑
Moon in Capricorn

We have reached the end of another journey! We can validate our own achievements and pack up our present to further develop our consciousness in 2025. I wish you the best cycle to come of your entire existence!.See you on the other side of this portal, and so long, my loves!

DREAM LIST

IN 2025 I WILL ...

2023

JANUARY

M	T	W	T	F	S	S
						1
2	3	4	5	6	**7**	**8**
9	10	11	12	13	**14**	**15**
16	17	18	19	20	**21**	**22**
23	24	25	26	27	**28**	**29**
30	31					

FEBRUARY

M	T	W	T	F	S	S
		1	2	3	**4**	**5**
6	7	8	9	10	**11**	**12**
13	14	15	16	17	**18**	**19**
20	21	22	23	24	**25**	**26**
27	28					

MARCH

M	T	W	T	F	S	S
		1	2	3	**4**	**5**
6	7	8	9	10	**11**	**12**
13	14	15	16	17	**18**	**19**
20	21	22	23	24	**25**	**26**
27	28	29	30	31		

APRIL

M	T	W	T	F	S	S
					1	**2**
3	4	5	6	7	**8**	**9**
10	11	12	13	14	**15**	**16**
17	18	19	20	21	**22**	**23**
24	25	26	27	28	**29**	**30**

MAY

M	T	W	T	F	S	S
1	2	3	4	5	**6**	**7**
8	9	10	11	12	**13**	**14**
15	16	17	18	19	**20**	**21**
22	23	24	25	26	**27**	**28**
29	30	31				

JUNE

M	T	W	T	F	S	S
			1	2	**3**	**4**
5	6	7	8	9	**10**	**11**
12	13	14	15	16	**17**	**18**
19	20	21	22	23	**24**	**25**
26	27	28	29	30		

JULY

M	T	W	T	F	S	S
					1	**2**
3	4	5	6	7	**8**	**9**
10	11	12	13	14	**15**	**16**
17	18	19	20	21	**22**	**23**
24	25	26	27	28	**29**	**30**
31						

AUGUST

M	T	W	T	F	S	S
	1	2	3	4	**5**	**6**
7	8	9	10	11	**12**	**13**
14	15	16	17	18	**19**	**20**
21	22	23	24	25	**26**	**27**
28	29	30	31			

SEPTEMBER

M	T	W	T	F	S	S
				1	**2**	**3**
4	5	6	7	8	**9**	**10**
11	12	13	14	15	**16**	**17**
18	19	20	21	22	**23**	**24**
25	26	27	28	29	**30**	

OCTOBER

M	T	W	T	F	S	S
						1
2	3	4	5	6	**7**	**8**
9	10	11	12	13	**14**	**15**
16	17	18	19	20	**21**	**22**
23	24	25	26	27	**28**	**29**
30	31					

NOVEMBER

M	T	W	T	F	S	S
		1	2	3	**4**	**5**
6	7	8	9	10	**11**	**12**
13	14	15	16	17	**18**	**19**
20	21	22	23	24	**25**	**26**
27	28	29	30			

DECEMBER

M	T	W	T	F	S	S
				1	**2**	**3**
4	5	6	7	8	**9**	**10**
11	12	13	14	15	**16**	**17**
18	19	20	21	22	**23**	**24**
25	26	27	28	29	**30**	**31**

2025

JANUARY

M	T	W	T	F	S	S
		1	2	3	4	5
6	7	8	9	10	11	12
13	14	15	16	17	18	19
20	21	22	23	24	25	26
27	28	29	30	31		

FEBRUARY

M	T	W	T	F	S	S
					1	2
3	4	5	6	7	8	9
10	11	12	13	14	15	16
17	18	19	20	21	22	23
24	25	26	27	28		

MARCH

M	T	W	T	F	S	S
					1	2
3	4	5	6	7	8	9
10	11	12	13	14	15	16
17	18	19	20	21	22	23
24	25	26	27	28	29	30
31						

APRIL

M	T	W	T	F	S	S
	1	2	3	4	5	6
7	8	9	10	11	12	13
14	15	16	17	18	19	20
21	22	23	24	25	26	27
28	29	30				

MAY

M	T	W	T	F	S	S
			1	2	3	4
5	6	7	8	9	10	11
12	13	14	15	16	17	18
19	20	21	22	23	24	25
26	27	28	29	30	31	

JUNE

M	T	W	T	F	S	S
						1
2	3	4	5	6	7	8
9	10	11	12	13	14	15
16	17	18	19	20	21	22
23	24	25	26	27	28	29
30						

JULY

M	T	W	T	F	S	S
	1	2	3	4	5	6
7	8	9	10	11	12	13
14	15	16	17	18	19	20
21	22	23	24	25	26	27
28	29	30	31			

AUGUST

M	T	W	T	F	S	S
				1	2	3
4	5	6	7	8	9	10
11	12	13	14	15	16	17
18	19	20	21	22	23	24
25	26	27	28	29	30	31

SEPTEMBER

M	T	W	T	F	S	S
1	2	3	4	5	6	7
8	9	10	11	12	13	14
15	16	17	18	19	20	21
22	23	24	25	26	27	28
29	30					

OCTOBER

M	T	W	T	F	S	S
		1	2	3	4	5
6	7	8	9	10	11	12
13	14	15	16	17	18	19
20	21	22	23	24	25	26
27	28	29	30	31		

NOVEMBER

M	T	W	T	F	S	S
					1	2
3	4	5	6	7	8	9
10	11	12	13	14	15	16
17	18	19	20	21	22	23
24	25	26	27	28	29	30

DECEMBER

M	T	W	T	F	S	S
1	2	3	4	5	6	7
8	9	10	11	12	13	14
15	16	17	18	19	20	21
22	23	24	25	26	27	28
29	30	31				

FORGET ME NOT

WWW / APP LOGIN

PASSWORD EMAIL

WWW / APP LOGIN

PASSWORD EMAIL

WWW / APP LOGIN

PASSWORD EMAIL

WWW / APP LOGIN

PASSWORD EMAIL

WWW / APP LOGIN

PASSWORD EMAIL

WWW / APP LOGIN

PASSWORD EMAIL

WWW / APP LOGIN

PASSWORD EMAIL

WWW / APP LOGIN

PASSWORD EMAIL

WWW / APP LOGIN

PASSWORD EMAIL

ANA•LEO

THE ASTROLOGY DIARY

2024

Dream, Plan and Manifest!

Every day, Ana Leo looks at the horizon in search of new directions, discoveries and answers.

A yogini and student of Kabbalah, she is intuitive and curious about hermeticism and occult sciences; she sees in the art of Astrology a powerful way to promote self-knowledge and human development.

Graduated in Design and post-graduated in History, she studied Astrology at the Faculty of Astrological Studies, in Oxford. She took classes with renowned teachers and was a disciple of the most important Astrologer in Brazil: Mr. Zeferino Costa.

In 2019, she launched her Astrology Diary for the first time, a true guide to manifest your dreams in real life. In the same year, she studied Astronomy at the Royal Observatory in Greenwich, London, and since then, she has not stopped traveling the world.

Spending her time between Brazil, England, Portugal, Panama and Argentina, she seeks inspiration and information, to add to her personalized services. With Astral Charts and Tarot Readings, she's always attentive to the planetary aspects of the moment, the qualities of each person and the characteristics of each group she serves.

YouTube.com/analeo
Instagram @analeo